Patricia Gosling is a retired psychoanalytical psychotherapist in the British Independent tradition. She has a background in Medicine, Marital Counselling, Clinical Theology and the hurly-burly of family life.

For fifty years Patricia has been a member of the Religious Society of Friends (Quakers).

Other books by Patricia Gosling:
A Curious Eye (2006)
Fatal Flaws (2012)

Autobiography
A Time of Transition (2011)

Poetry
Loving and Loss (2009)
Enduring (2014)

Front Cover:

Detail from *Presence in the Wood* by Nigel Done

The Long Perspective

Patricia Gosling

The White Hart

Published by
White Hart Books
Rode, England
hart@gosmob.eu

for

Ceri

last but never least

also remembering

Dr. Dorothy Speed

innovative and intriguing professional

encouraging sounding-board

irreplaceable friend

Contents

The fall of empires
What has Christensen to say?

Introduction

When human beings - the naked apes - first descended from the trees, we were extremely vulnerable. Our chief asset was our high intelligence, which we have subsequently used to good effect. The downside of that intelligence has been a conscious awareness of our vulnerability, and of the inevitability of dying. We had acquired existential anxiety.

We have found all sorts of ways of managing that anxiety, some more creative than others. The use of alcohol and mood-changing drugs has a long history in many cultures. The observation and search for the rhythms, regularities and patterning of our world has been compulsive and immensely fruitful. When we were hunter-gatherers, it aided the search for food and shelter. It then enabled us to flourish as agriculturalists. Latterly it has fuelled our scientific explorations.

We have a need to make sense of the world and our experiences in it. The alternative is too disturbing; it feels like chaos — threatening disintegration and madness. Where we do not know, or cannot know, we make up stories to fill the void. It is as if any story is better than none. This is how religions begin.

Story-telling to entertain or to fill in the gaps of not-knowing is one thing. When those stories come to be believed in as 'The Truth' they can become dangerous and a source of rigidity and conflict.

Equally dangerous are the fantasies we construct for ourselves to relieve the anxiety of not-knowing, without being aware that that is what we are doing. I cannot but think that much political theorising comes into this category. One can flatter it by calling it idealism, but when it has little connection to the actual world, it is potentially dangerous. Much economic thinking is equally a flight of fantasy which ignores manifest reality. People as rational optimisers ... I think not!

The following book is an attempt at telling the story of social change in the UK in recent decades. It has been prompted by a growing, widespread sense of discomfort and uncertainty, the collapse of hitherto trustworthy institutions, and a crisis of faith - faith in the religious sense, but also faith in the health, identity and stability of our national community.

It is also a plea for the recognition of — and respect for — our basic biology. Our innate drives and limitations are the heritage of our evolutionary history, and they will not be denied. Attempting to do so is to invite disaster.

I am aware that running throughout this story are two vital threads whose twitching tails lassoed me in my teenage years. They have both continued to infuse my experience, and are an integral part of my thinking and my identity.

The first is a perception of the nature of the universe which might be called religious, or more fashionably, spiritual. My experience of the numinous came unbidden — wordless and mind-blowing. I subsequently found that such experience was shared by many others, both contemporary and in the past, and coming from widely different cultural backgrounds. Somewhat to my surprise, I now find that perception blends seamlessly into current scientific theorising, although the language is different.

The second thread is my essentially biological and psychoanalytic understanding of human beings and their development. I belong to the Freudian school of thought, and to that group who have come to be known as the Independent Tradition. There are many practitioners in this stream whose ideas have resonated with my own, and who have further stimulated my thinking; but I feel particularly grateful that I met up with the writings of D.W.Winnicott — paediatrician and psychoanalyst extraordinaire — so early in adult life.

Two psychoanalysts from outside that tradition have also hugely influenced my understanding — the American Thomas Ogden[1], and the French Janine Chasseguet-Smirgel[2].

Ogden's conceptualisation of the three polarities of psychic functioning, and Chasseguet-Smirgel's thinking about perversion, each developed out of clinical work with individual patients. I too found their ideas helpful and transformative in that context. Only later did I gradually come to suspect that they might also be relevant to the functioning of the larger social group.

I am amused that, after so many years of psychoanalysis being 'out in the cold' as far as mainstream scientists were con-

---

1 Ogden, Thomas (1989) *The Primitive Edge of Experience* Aronson. Ogden's thinking has been much influenced by that of D.W.Winnicott.

2 Chasseguet-Smirgel, Janine (1984) *Creativity and Perversion* foreword by Otto Kernberg.

cerned, neuropsychology — with the aid of brain scanning — is now confirming many of Freud's original speculations.

It has always felt important to me to integrate my experience and understanding into a coherent whole. It has been a lifetime's adventure, and is ongoing still. The following chapters are stories of that adventure.

1. War

The 1914-18 conflict was supposed to be 'the war to end all wars.' Sadly, the serious mismanagement of the subsequent peace made the 1939-45 sequel inevitable. The punitive reparations imposed upon the defeated led to social chaos in Germany, and the emergence of a charismatic but deeply pathological leader with intolerable ambitions.

Since that time we, in our corner of Europe, have been fortunate in living in peace. However, we have watched our soldiers go off to fight in Korea, in Vietnam, in Bosnia, in Iraq and recently in Afghanistan — with ebbing public support.

The Israel/Palestinian tensions rumble painfully on, Syria is being devastated by its civil war, and the Middle East generally is struggling with a state of conflict within the Muslim community between Suni and Shia factions. Russia has yet to come to terms with its loss of empire, and its neighbours' reluctance to return to the fold. A peaceful world it is not!

What is war about?

In the current news headlines, one of our soldiers is in process of being prosecuted for the murder of an Afghan soldier. Meanwhile our Prime Minister, David Cameron, who is visiting Sri Lanka *(August 2014)* is demanding that those responsible for war crimes in the recent civil war there should be brought to justice. In that brutal conflict, many have disappeared without trace. The distress of their loved ones, as revealed on television, is painful to behold.

Behind both these events is the assumption that war can be fought observing certain rules of decency. We have the Geneva convention which states what is acceptable and what is not. We pride ourselves on the discipline and professionalism of our own army — rightly so.

Nonetheless, at times people behave badly — of course. War is about murdering other people. Once society licenses that activity, it licenses the emergence of our innate aggression and destructive capacity. To keep it under some measure of control has always been a major task of the military leadership.

The Society of Friends has historically maintained a peace witness, and has asserted that the solution is to 'take away the occasion of war'. In the current climate that witness is ever more urgent.

As living creatures, and as social mammals, we are driven by two innate instincts. The first is to ensure our individual survival by finding the necessary food and shelter; the second is to ensure the survival of our species by reproducing and nurturing our young.

In our early pre-history as hunter-gatherers it was the men's role to guard the territory which provided the food — the plants and the game — and in which the females were safe to bear and nurture the young. The major threat would have been from other animals. Subsequently, as the population grew, the nearby presence of other human groups impinged.

This became more so as humans took up farming and settled in specific areas — their homesteads.

The more successful and prosperous a certain group became, the more vulnerable they became to the envious attacks of outsiders. We can still see in the landscape the remnants of Iron Age hill-forts which bear witness to this phase of human history.

As the pressure of population grew, the more it seemed necessary to develop a class of warriors to defend the group's assets. In this way there developed a privileged class, and a hierarchy of importance, leadership and the battles for power within the group. It became an increasingly patriarchal organisation.

The group's social organisation became distorted in the service of maintaining a fighting band of warriors. Its values became military values. Its educational system was designed to promote those values. It neglected or gave little status to those activities which did not support this perspective.

All kinds of male activities developed around the war function — the forging of weapons, the skills of archery, horsemanship, learning to fight in armour and the tournaments in which it was practised. The greater size and strength of the male was significant and needed as long as weapons powered by human muscle were the norm. This began to change with the development of cannon in the 14th century; but military horses were still being kept behind the battle lines as late as 1917.

Meanwhile the fundamental activities and values of the females became ever more secondary. The myths of idealisation — Romance — grew, but the reality all too often condemned them to be pawns in the power games of others. One saw a resurgence of these attitudes in Hitler's Germany when the explicit function of women was just to produce the next generation of soldiers.

While more and more of the group's resources were used to pursue fighting, going to war enabled some men to become rich. Combatants stole and looted from the defeated; wealthy captives were held to ransom. War was a risky business but the rewards were potentially enormous. A cult of the hero — bravery, honour, patriotism — developed in order to boost the soldiers' courage, and to deny the reality of what was actually going on. The powerful bought or stole large tracts of land which became an ongoing source of wealth, while in return they were expected to provide fighting men when required. They became the aristocracy, and we still have the remnants of that class system today.

Where are we now? The Age of Chivalry is long past. The heroic knight in shining armour was toppled by the use of gunpowder. Centuries later, even so, the number of men engaged in war was still a small proportion of the male population, and armies were largely composed of professional soldiers.

Napoleon changed all that with his *levee en masse*. His wanton use of manpower was devastating in its consequences for France, leaving too few young men to fulfil their roles within the family and to work the land. Civilians could no longer leave war to the professionals; and more recently the whole population has become at risk.

Even in Jane Austen's day, it was still possible to purchase a commission in the army or navy, and (if one survived) return home with one's fortune increased. Nowadays war is different: for winners and losers alike it has become an expensive business.

Before 1914, Germany was a prosperous country with a thriving industry, and scientifically at the spearhead of developing knowledge. By 1918 it was exhausted. France took the remnants of its industry in reparation, and wasn't until after a devastating depression and the emergence of the Hitler regime that prosperity began to return. (The reparations proved to be a white elephant. France was lumbered with out-of-date factories and equipment; Germany had to re-build from scratch and ended up with state-of-the-art manufacturing capacity.)

In 1914 England was a wealthy country with a vast empire. In the 19th century it had about 80% of all the manufacturing capacity in the world. By 1945 it was bankrupt, with the last vestiges of empire slipping away to independence. Since then, our capacity for destruction has increased vastly, and with it the escalating expense to fuel it.

There has always been a fall-out affecting subsequent generations. In my own small family, an uncle had half of his face blown away. It was repaired to some degree by pioneer surgeon Archibald McIndoe using animal bone, which later became cancerous. A grandfather's lungs and heart were damaged, leading to chronic ill-health and an early death. A father was so traumatised by his experience as a teenager on a hospital ship that he had a mental breakdown. He survived, against the odds, when the submarine he was too ill to join was lost, with half the crew drowned. Each of these events distorted the lives of those close to them, and added to the difficulties of the younger generations.

9

One hopes that in time the traumas can be compensated for, but it takes a very long time for families to recover from the losses.

The truth is that we can no longer afford war. In its final days the Soviet Union was spending 27% of its Gross National Product on armaments, in an attempt to compete with the USA. It was unsustainable and it collapsed.

Today the USA spends vast sums on its military, more than the next eleven countries (including China and Russia) added together, but cannot afford to provide a decent health service for its poorest people.

The original purpose of going to war to benefit the tribe has long been lost. Much ingenuity and effort has gone into developing weapons over the years. The human talent for technological invention has stimulated creativity in this area as in so many others. Now our weapons are so destructive that we cannot afford the devastation they bring. The potential use of nuclear bombs threatens to destroy the environment on which we depend for our very existence. The ongoing effects from Chernobyl, and the recent Japanese nuclear power station disaster, has given us enough of a foretaste of the possible horrors. The fall-out from nuclear war would poison much of the landscape for innumerable generations to come. We have no right to do that.

War has become obsolete

What next? There are certain issues within society which are an ongoing source of trouble and need to be addressed. We have to find alternative outlets for aggression, and for the power battles between dominant males for their place in the hierarchy.

There is a particular problem for young men at this time, which is reflected in the high suicide rate within this age group. We need to find activities that will occupy and satisfy them, and which will make good use of their abundant energies. We have to give them a purpose in the wider society other than as fighters. We have to find them roles which give them a sense of significance and value.

- Active participation in sport does this for some, but its commercialisation has not been beneficial.
- Apprenticeships tie them into the world of the mature men of the tribe, and give them a hierarchy to climb; but at present these offer too low a status and reward to be attractive.
- Higher education has historically performed a similar function, but the current situation where a degree no longer guarantees a job is demoralising.

There is a case to be made for the equivalent of the two years military conscription of yesteryear, in which the young could be taught useful skills and do valuable community work. It would also enable those trapped in social ghettos to escape the pathological culture of such places. (David Cameron has begun such a scheme in a very small way, and hopefully it might be a precursor of something larger.)

As girls increasingly adopt a male lifestyle and values, perhaps they too need a similar scheme. The old-style nursing training provided it for some.

There is one task that all of us need to tackle. We have to come to terms with otherness and difference in peoples. We have to improve our ability to negotiate with those differences and accept them.

Firstly we need to re-instate the boundary between private and public. This has been seriously eroded in recent years as electronic communication becomes ever easier and cheaper. The press has been guilty of unacceptable intrusion into people's private lives, while others conduct intimate conversations via the inter-net revealing details which they may later come to regret. Some have recently been sending pornographic pictures of themselves on Facebook.

The concept of what is appropriate public behaviour has become eroded. It is the teenagers and young adults who mostly fail to distinguish between public and private life, because they are seeking for public confirmation of their significance. However, we all need privacy in order to develop our real selves, our inner core of being. Exhibitionism is a poor and shallow substitute.

Although it has not been fashionable in liberal circles to admit such feelings, we need to accept the reality that we all feel more comfortable with our own kind, our own clan. We all tend to, and indeed may consciously choose to, continue the patterns of our childhood within our own homes and families; and we need the privacy which will allow us to do that. At the same time we live in a wider world with its own social norms. These have to be generally accepted and respected as the price of living in a civilised society. Immigrants in particular need to understand this.

In the UK we have had a lot of experience of this over the centuries as the various different cultural groups have learned — painfully — to live together. Those who have 'migrated' between the social classes have also had to learn such skills. The large scale immigration of recent years is another phase of this cultural phenomenon. The founders of the USA understood the problem, and set out consciously to manage it with a considerable, if only partial, measure of success.

The boundaries between 'us' and 'them' which used to be drawn around the tribe, then later around the nation, are now in our midst. All war is destructive, and civil war most of all. We have to learn ways, not of denying, nor of destroying, but of living with difference. There is a price to be paid, but it is nothing like as high as the long-term destructiveness we inflict on each other when we fight.

We need to cultivate social attitudes which sees war as social failure and breakdown, and warlike behaviour as a source of shame not fame. Von Clausewitz memorably said, 'War is the continuation of politics by other means' — but he went on to add that 'it is to politics that it must return'. We no longer have any other option. We have to 'take away the occasion of war' if we are to survive as a species.

2. Getting started

The human animal is a long time a-growing. Its immaturity extends over roughly a fifth of its life-span. Some of this time is occupied by that peculiarly human episode — the latency period — when, so-to-speak, the individual's emotional path is put on hold and its energies are taken up in relating to its social environment and, in particular, its peer-group.

Even when born, it is still very immature and vulnerable, totally dependent on its carers, in sharp contrast to many other young mammals who struggle to their feet within minutes of birth.

The baby needs to be expelled from the womb at a certain point because of the size of its head and the brain inside it. If it were any larger, it would never manage the transition. As it is, that brain keeps growing for some time after birth, and the sutures uniting the cranial bones do not fuse until it is two years old.

How does this immature creature experience the world at this point? Recent work suggests that consciousness is already developing while the foetus is still in situ. It is aware of music, of other sounds outside the mother, of her movements and heart-beat. It probably feels warm, comfortable, contained and safe — all the conditions we try to create for the newly born on arrival. That is the basic floor of sensory experience; and we try to re-create it every night when we go to sleep.

The first transition

At some deep physiological level, it seems that the decision of birth is a mutual negotiation between mother and infant; the child is ready to make the change and there is a drop in the mother's hormonal level. We may like to think that the child has no later memory of this momentous event, but there is evidence to the contrary. I suspect that how this first transition is experienced lays down the pattern for that individual's subsequent major life changes — whether welcomed with enthusiasm, dreaded, avoided, accompanied by anxiety; whether actively engaged with or passively suffered.

Birth via the normal channel must inevitably be a stressful, if not shocking, experience to some degree. All that noise and light; air entering the lungs; having things poked into one's orifices; being handled, washed, wrapped up in fabric. No wonder babies complain! They are at the mercy of stimuli which have as yet no meaning. They are 'trapped in a non-subjective world of thoughts and feelings experienced in terms of frightening and protective things that simply happen, and that cannot be thought about or interpreted.' [1] Good postnatal care aims to minimise this disruptive experience, and soothe.

It has been suggested that a difficult birth experience can have long-term effects on the subsequent development of the individual. Some have linked it to a schizoid personality — a withdrawal from inter-personal relationships into an intellectual inner world. Others have seen the genesis of male homo-

---

[1] A quotation from psychoanalyst Thomas Ogden.

15

sexuality here, with its turning away from the Woman as a source of unbearable pain.

At the same time, one wonders if the apparently easier option of birth by Caesarian section has its effect. Does it produce babies who have a more passive reaction to life? And what of babies born under the influence of powerful pain-killing drugs? Is there any connection here with the current epidemic of recreational drug use? Certainly we have learned that babies not born vaginally miss out on acquiring some important micro-organisms. We also now know that being born prematurely is likely to lead to a reduced expectation of life-span and above-average morbidity.

Growth begins

Most of us survive the uncomfortable shock of our arrival as separate human beings, and begin the lengthy growth process ahead of us. We learn gradually to make sense of what is happening to us and around us; we build up a coherent picture of the world in which we find ourselves; we build up relationships with others who care for and support us; we learn to walk, to talk, and the skills of managing our environment. Hopefully we also learn to wait, to be aware of others, and to consider them as well as ourselves. We learn to tolerate disappointment and ambivalent feelings; we survive crises, and learn that we can. It is a long process, and not without grief. As we acquire some sense of time, we begin to gain some historical perspective. It has been called 'the depressive position' — not perhaps the best term for what is a normal and healthy stance. (Perhaps 'depressive' because we come to accept some of our own personal limitations — never welcome!) I prefer to call it the 'stage of concern'.

Ideally, as we grow up, we need and get a lot of support and encouragement. At the beginning our subjective world is either heaven or hell; later our mood swings become moderated. It is never easy. If we get, not help, but too much criticism, too rigid expectations, harsh punishment, then it inhibits our capacity to grow. What can then develop is 'a form of isolation from one's bodily sensations, and from the immediacy of one's lived experience, leaving one devoid of spontaneity and aliveness.'[2] We are then talking of a depressed human being — and a depressed child is in serious trouble.

---

[2]Also quoted from psychoanalyst Thomas Ogden.

3. Social modality: the balancing act

These modes of being that we experience in our immaturity are the building blocks of our subsequent life. From our early sensory floor we develop our embodied emotional and sexual life; what we have come to associate with Right-brain activity.

Out of the concretely experienced impingements of the outside world, we learn to deal with and manage that world, and to make some kind of sense of it. We develop our Left-brain activities, we become managers, engineers, thinkers, scientists.

From the stage of concern we develop our relationships with others, our family and social networks, our concern for the common good and wider humanity.

A 'normal' healthy life is lived somewhere in the middle of all this, drawing on these different modes of being as appropriate, developing them in parallel. Psychopathology develops when we fall too much for too long in one direction. Then we become self-indulgent, addicted and perverse, or paranoid-schizoid [1] and rigid, or depressed. When we become stuck in

---

[1] Paranoid/schizoid. A term from psychoanalytical Object Relations Theory. It was first used by Melanie Klein to describe the phase of development of an infant between birth and six months old. It describes the child's attempts to defend itself against the impingements of the outside world

that one way of being, then we are in trouble. Our growth as a full human being is stalled. We need help.

This is the pattern of our individual development, determined by our innate biology and then modified by our subsequent experience.

Social animals that we are, there are similar patterns at work in our group life. The dynamics of small groups have received some attention, and valuable insights have been achieved. The sheer scale of larger social dynamics makes study difficult, not only because of the number of individuals in any contemporary society, but also because of the time-scale involved.

Politics, which purports to study these things, tends to have all too short a time-scale. Too much of historical research has concentrated on politics, monarchs and wars, though the lives of ordinary folk are now beginning to receive some attention. The changes I have in mind operate over longer than a single life-span, making observation problematic.

I think I can detect phases of social and cultural life which exhibit patterns similar to those we see in individual functioning.

The Romantic movement in Europe was surely an attempt to keep in touch with the sensory and emotional 'floor' of our being. *La Vie de Boheme* was seductive, especially to the young.

Protestantism, and the Enlightenment was an attempt to make sense of a world battered by events impinging on the social order. It encouraged the Scientific Revolution, which has bought enormous changes to our society.

The Liberalism of the 19th century, which fuelled subsequent socialist thinking, was a reflection of the concern of caring individuals for the less fortunate in our society. In an earlier age, that role had been performed by the Church, before the Reformation swept away the monastic institutions in this country.

It is apparent that, whether thinking of the individual or of the wider society, the three different modalities have both a positive and a negative aspect.

For the individual, the sensory/ Romantic mode makes for a sensuous experience of life, open to sensory impressions from outside and instinctual and sexual impulses from within. It connects with our basic biological endowment, and with the creativity that drives it. It is the foundation of artistic expression, interpersonal warmth and much imaginative play.

It can become negative if the other modes are not functioning adequately, leading to an increasingly desperate search for sensory satisfaction — in food, in drugs, in sexual behaviour, in the acquisition of material objects. Such behaviour tends to have an addictive quality, needing ever more sensory stimulation to satisfy the insatiable need.

In the wider culture, if the Romantic movement becomes dominant, the group becomes hedonistic and deals inadequately with the harsher aspects of reality. In practice this tends to occur to a certain class within society at the expense of the rest, who are treated as inferior beings.

These inferior beings may be slaves as in Ancient Greece and Rome. In pre-revolutionary France, the aristocracy lived in-

dulgent, narcissistic lives, while the common people were seriously impoverished by the unfair taxation system.

In England of the 18th and 19th centuries, the life-style of the
upper classes, the 'ton', was only sustained by an army of servants. The conditions of life of the working class was such that
they did indeed seem to belong to a different race — they
tended to be physically smaller and less well-developed.
When men came to be enlisted into the army for the 1914-18
conflict, there was some dismay at the lack of fitness and level
of morbidity amongst the potential recruits.

The danger is that the hedonistic class becomes increasingly
infantilised and inadequate in its dealings with the real world.
The search for sensual satisfaction becomes increasingly difficult to satisfy; addiction and perversion flourish.

Then we see the wider social development of typically perverse behaviour. Here I am using the term 'perverse' in a
technical, psychoanalytic sense, based on the insights of
Janine Chasseguet-Smirgel. She sees it as a universal human
tendency, and derives it from a failure of the child to grapple
with the challenges of the Oedipal phase of development. Instead the individual retreats into an earlier anal phase of relating to the outside world, maintaining its phantasy of om-
nipotence, and the inexhaustibility of supplies (food, money,
clothes etc.) It denies the difference between the sexes, between the generations, attempts to obliterate all boundaries
and restrictions, and denies the meaning of history.

Socially we have been living in a perverse phase, marked by a
retreat from reality, erosion of boundaries, a denial of difference, an assumption of inexhaustible resources, a negation of
meaning and of history, the triumph of fantasy in inappropri-

ate areas — as we have seen in the banking industry. Such behaviour has been rampant in our society in recent decades.

Struggle against chaos

During that phase of infantile development which psychoanalysts talk of as the paranoid/schizoid phase, the small person lives in a world of concretely experienced impingements which he struggles to react to and make sense of. A good mother brings the world to her infant in such a way that some kind of order and routine comes into existence, initially outside and then within the child. If the infant's world is too chaotic to make any kind of sense, then madness threatens.

Some people seem content to live their adult lives in a state of 'suchness', adopting a pragmatic, accepting stance in which they get on with the tasks in front of them as best they can without asking many questions.

Apparently, according to Thomas Cahill[2] the Sumerians, our earliest civilised forebears, had no sense of history. They believed that the world in which they lived had been given them by the 'gods', and was and would be unchanging. They had no sense of development and evolution such as is central to our own perspective on human life. This did not prevent them from developing the first cities, having a flourishing agriculture, and inventing writing — on clay tablets. They clearly had sophisticated building techniques; they had technology, but they had no science. They had learned from experience how to do certain things, but they had not developed a coherent system of ideas as to why their techniques worked.

---

[2] Thomas Cahill (1998) *The Gifts of the Jews* Doubleday

Hans Küng, the Roman Catholic theologian, in a sensitive and sympathetic passage about the religious beliefs of the Australian aborigines, describes a similar mind-set[3].

Living in a world of suchness, when things become difficult a basic reaction is to blame someone, something, outside one's self — a mental technique we know as splitting and projection. Small children do it all the time; it protects their fragile self-esteem and the pain of feeling incompetent and foolish. (Naughty chair for hurting my toe!) When the mechanism persists in the adult we call it paranoia. It leads individuals and even whole societies to fight each other. It leads to war.

Making sense of it all

There are those in any society who continue to function in this way. Others want to make more sense of their experience, to develop some kind of ordering of their thoughts. We see here the beginnings of intellectual life, the development of the thinkers, the philosophers, the scientists who have brought such fruitful insights into our culture.

Protestantism and the Enlightenment, and the change of thinking they brought with them, were attempts to make sense of a world battered by events impinging on the social order. These thinkers encouraged the development of the Scientific Revolution which has brought enormous changes to our society. We nowadays give them acclaim — rightly — but they all came much later than the pragmatic 'doers', the fettlers who developed the technology of house-building, cooking, weaving, agricultural practice, metal-working long before

---

[3] Küng, Hans (2002) *Tracing The Way*

science existed. We knew how to make laminated steel swords a thousand years before we had a scientific explanation of why the technique worked.

In a society which is distorted by an over-development of this modality, there are a number of dangers. One is that too much value is placed upon the 'doing' without proper consideration of the possible consequences. Because we can do something does not mean we should. We banned the use of mustard gas in warfare; nuclear bombs remain a potential threat. We can increase our fishing catch by dredging the sea bottom, but if we continue to do so we shall destroy the fishing stocks we depend on.

We have come to recognise that this modality operates from Left-brain activity, in contrast with the Right-brain activity which is concerned with sensory stimulation, emotions and instinctual drive and hence with the Romantic modality.

This is a danger attendant upon an over-dominance of Left-brain activity over Right[4]. We get out of touch with our sensory mode, or allow it to become denigrated. In doing so we lose our sense of wonderment, our poetry, our sense of the numinous. We create a soulless kind of existence.

The retreat from sensual and sexual involvement, from disturbing powerful feelings, into the safe, calm world of the intellect, can be very seductive. It appears to give relief from intolerable internal tensions, and promises a way of understanding and managing the threatening outer world.

---

[4] McGilchrist, Iain (2009) *The Master & His Emissary* Yale

Catholic Christianity encouraged this in its monastic and eremitical traditions. The Reformation produced singularly joyless and punitive varieties of Protestantism such as Calvinism. The Jansenism of the Roman Church was in similar mode. Such life-denying trends can be found in other major religions also — in some forms of both Buddhism and Hinduism.

It can lead to an ideal of Man as Robot, such as the *Star Trek* television character Mr. Spock. One thinks of classical Sparta — a society totally devoted to warfare — of the goose-stepping Nazi cohorts, of well-trained soldiers on parade with their stiff bodies and stiff movements. It can lead to an over-valuation of the military virtues, and the 'stiff upper lip' emotional response. At its worst, the culturally encouraged inhibition of emotional empathy allows human beings to do dreadful things to one another — to torture, to create death camps — and feel justified in the doing. Normal human feeling is experienced as deeply unwelcome and persecutory.

At its worst, an unholy alliance can develop as those benumbed of feeling desperately try to hang on to it in a form which becomes sado-masochistic. We see this in the disturbed adolescent, in desperate retreat from the pain of living, who takes to self-harming. They say that by inflicting pain upon themselves, it helps them to feel more alive.

We meet with relationships which remain intact though full of pain. Sometimes the pain is that of domestic violence, sometimes it is purely verbal. One thinks of the play, *Who's Afraid Of Virginia Woolf?*[5] It was such a success because it represented a certain reality which the audience recognised. Mar-

---

[5] Albee, Edward (1962) *Who's Afraid of Virginia Woolf?*

riages in which the parties continually snipe bitchily at each other are not uncommon, and they often resist well-meaning attempts to break them up.

When this sado-masochism is acted out in the wider public arena, the results are horrific. In our time we have witnessed it in Nazi Germany, in the USSR, in Saddam Hussein's Iraq, in the Cambodia of the Khmer Rouge. History is full of it; it is nothing new. It is hope distorted into hellish destruction.

The stage of concern is a relative late development in the life of the small individual. If the mother and baby have bonded well, the infant is about eight months old before it realises that the good mother who makes it feel warm and comfortable, and the bad mother who fails to appear at his demand, are one and the same person — and it is not a welcome perception! It is not until around thirty-six months of age that the small child has a sufficiently stable sense of its own separate identity that he can fully accept the reality — that mother is not under his control! At the same time, one hopes, he has learned to accept that there are other people inhabiting the world they share — father, siblings, neighbours — who also demand her attention; and that his needs do not always have priority!

Hopefully, these other beings have their positive qualities which mediate the affront to his narcissism, and help to provide other positive input to his young life. Toddlers in the pre-school years need both loving encouragement, and firm boundaries. It is well-nigh impossible for one care-giver to do both. There is ample evidence that small boys with no father around tend to behave more aggressively, and are less willing to subsequently accept discipline. Since proto-sexuality is always with us, small girls who have had a man around to play and flirt with will find it easier to relate to the opposite sex later in life.

Pre-school and school proper are further challenges to the child's autocracy, but our innate sociability draws the child into relationship with its peers, and during the latency years these become dominant. Hopefully, by the time adolescence strikes, the child will have learned to share, learned to cooperate with others, learned to care for and feel concerned for its nearest and dearest, learned some basic social skills.

It is from this group of well-nurtured children that sound citizens are formed. It is they who will do the necessary work of society, facilitating others, founding their own families, serving the wider community. Much of what they do will be taken for granted, unrecognised, unsung; but whatever their level of achievement and acclaim in the outside world, they will be experienced as good and decent people, reliable, a safe pair of hands.

The safety and sanity of our society depends on these men and women. If we demand too much of them, if the other modalities are not there to balance society's need, the burden can become too great. The initial reaction is to increase the concerned and caring mode. In times past, religion has often been invoked to encourage people to stay with it. If encouragement is not enough, the pressure can become desperate and bullying. One saw this in some of the religiosity of the 19th century.

Depressive societies

Just as individuals can become depressed as they attempt to struggle with the painful realities of life, so can societies.

There is not here a retreat into the ivory tower of the well-developed schizoid solution. [6] There is however a gradual shutting down into inhibition, repression and increasing rigidity. There is a lack of spontaneity, immediacy and aliveness. Life becomes grey and dreary; there is no space for the inner child to play. Instead, a semblance of life is attempted by ever more control and micro-management — which doesn't work!

After the slide into perversion of Regency society, a resurgence of the depressive mode of concern was welcomed, and a healthy reaction. However, society was under other stresses at that time from the surge of industrialisation and its impact. The Industrial Revolution — the introduction of machines to take the place of manual labour — was traumatic for many. Former agricultural labourers poured into the cities with their dependents, seeking work and the means to survive. If rural poverty had been tough, the over-crowding and squalor of the towns with their inadequate infra-structure made them a breeding ground for disease and criminality.

One has only to look at the early photographs of 19th century people, read the journals and correspondence of the affluent middle-classes, and get the flavour of the Evangelical Revival to appreciate that this was a deeply depressed society. The well-intentioned, concerned people did their best to mitigate

---

[6] Schizoid - literally split. Persons with this tendency are characterised by a lack of interest in social relationships, a tendency towards a solitary life-style, secretiveness and emotional coldness. They may simultaneously demonstrate a rich and elaborate internal fantasy world. Isaac Newton was such a personality.

some of the hardship of the dispossessed poor, but the impression is of little joy and spontaneity around.

To quote psychoanalyst Thomas Ogden, 'Collapse in the direction of the depressive pole involves a form of isolation from one's bodily sensations, and from the immediacy of one's lived experience, leaving one devoid of spontaneity and aliveness.'

That seems to me to describe all too well how life was for too many people in the latter part of the 19th century and well into the 20th.

If those overly concerned with containing and managing society's ills sometimes paid a high personal price, such people were invaluable in their activities on behalf of the less fortunate of their fellows. It was this group who worked for the abolition of slavery, for the laws which stopped children working in mines, being used as chimney sweeps. Where would the teaching and nursing professions be without them, the doctors, the police force, the social workers? They are the group who could be relied upon to bolster the infra-structure of the social order, not to turn their backs on what was uncomfortable and unwelcome in the social fabric. By forming groups — from the Fabian Society down to trade unions, professional organisations to the National Trust, they protected themselves from despair and burn-out, as well as gaining strength for their causes. A strong religious faith frequently under-pinned their endeavours.

A society that is functioning well needs these different kinds of people, and can accommodate and appreciate them.

In a society which is functioning well-enough, certain groups will exhibit the extreme modes of behaviour as described. The

Romantic/Bohemian life-style tends to be favoured by the artistic community, whose search for a way of living that feels emotionally and sensually real often leads them into experimentation — in relationships, in sexual behaviour, in the use of alcohol and drugs. If some of this community squander their time and talent, others will create things of merit — in painting, in writing, in the theatre.

The intellectual retreat from the impingements of a harsh world into an emotionally pallid ivory tower has fuelled our society's intellectual development. In times past, people of this temperament populated the Church, the monasteries, the universities. If some of their activities were sterile, some of it has stimulated and expanded our understanding of the world in which we live, and how it functions. It brought about the Enlightenment and the Scientific Revolution, and underpinned engineering with a rational, scientific, theoretical base.

It is only when one of these modes comes to dominate, at the expense of the rest, that trouble looms.

4. Leaders and leadership

People who embody the depressive/concerned mode are the glue which holds society together. If their activities are often barely noticed, they are sorely missed when gone. However, for the most part such people are not charismatic, lacking those narcissistic qualities which demands recognition above all else. When they find themselves in a position of power, they tend to be the power behind the throne, the consiglieri, the creators of policy, which they leave others to sell. Political life is littered with the names of able, intelligent men who dropped out of the game on some excuse — but one suspects because they could no longer tolerate the competitive jockeying for audience, the ill-mannered barrage of insult, which characterises so much of our political life.

However, it seems to be an innate characteristic of the human group that, when it is in difficulties, it looks to a charismatic leader — a Big Daddy — to get it out of trouble. The psychodynamic origin of this tendency is obvious; the child within is looking to the father-figure to rescue it. It is a natural response.

I suspect that a community's unconscious need for a charismatic leader is both powerful and atavistic. David G. Winter, the American psychologist who has done much work on reading the personalities of notable figures, has pointed out that the reputed greatness of an American president tends to correlate positively with his character trait of power-seeking. [1] It corresponds much less positively with his character trait for achievement of some ideal or social change. The former tend to enjoy exercising power, and the political manoeuvring necessary to maintain it. The latter, by contrast, become frustrated by the inevitable compromises of the role, and a sense of failure begins to dog them. Surprisingly, it is this group who are more likely to organise a coup, or install an authoritarian, anti-democratic regime in order to fulfil their ambitions.

Failing leaders

The down-side is that such natural leaders are not necessarily up to the task in hand. All too often they are themselves immature and narcissistic, seeking personal glory rather than the well-being of the group. All too often their grandiosity leads them into attempting impossible goals — Alexander the Great and Napoleon come to mind — or having achieved power, they cling to it and become repressive bullies.

The mistake is to believe that they are the cause of a society's problems when actually they are just a symptom. The Western democracies keep making this mistake, since they have not yet realised that a democratic society is a high cultural achievement, not a natural social order. We keep experiencing the deposition of a tyrant only for social chaos to follow. Recent examples are Saddam Hussein in Iraq and Colonel Gadafi in Libya.

In the 20th century Yugoslavia was held together under Marshal Tito, only to fall apart into warring Balkan factions after

---

[1] Winter, D. G. (2005) *J. of Personality* 73.3 Blackwell

his death. Whatever one feels about Russia's Putin, he has a difficult situation to manage following the collapse of the Soviet Empire.

Much Western criticism has been addressed to the current Chinese government for its harsh repressive actions against dissidents, but so far they are managing a major degree of social change without paying the price of social breakdown.

In a crisis a society needs a charismatic and effective leader — to rally the troops, to inspire hope and courage, to encourage acceptance of the inevitable hardships. We had one such in Winston Churchill in our time; we had one in Wellington in the fight against Napoleon; Queen Elizabeth I memorably roused her troops during the war with Spain, and we still thrill to the words of Shakespeare's young Henry V.

We also need the mechanisms for shedding them when the crisis is past! When the time comes for the dust to settle and for normal life to be resumed, they can be a menace. It is hard on them — they may feel they have not received their due deserts — but it is the sign of a mature society that it can manage the change without internal bloodshed. Successful war leaders and good peacetime leaders are different kinds of animal.

Monarchy

I suspect that kingship is the way the human tribe has institutionalised its need for Big Daddy. Although in recent years many countries have abolished their monarchies, they are then left vulnerable to take-over by pathological tyrants, or narcissistic but incompetent politicians. A few European countries, the UK among them, have achieved a remarkable compromise. We have an hereditary constitutional monarch with limited powers, who fulfils various important symbolic functions, and who embodies the soul of the nation. At the same time, we have an elected political leadership which can be changed as circumstances and society deems fit.

It is an arrangement which so far has worked very well. It should be cherished. It separates the Head of State from both the executive powers, and the military hierarchy, unlike the constitution of the US. It is interesting that it has enabled a woman to function as the symbolic leader as effectively as a man — in the UK and in the Netherlands.

One does not need to have a monarchy in order to separate the symbolic function from the executive. A president and a prime minister is an equally valid arrangement, and Ireland has been well served by this structure in recent years — again with women acting to good effect in the presidential role. However, preserving an existing monarchy gives a sense of historical continuity which has value for many, and acts as a force for stability.

5. The juggling act falters

Where are we in our society today? The 1914-18 war, with its mass carnage of men, destroyed much of the previous social order. The shortage of young men left a superfluity of women whose prospects were sadly diminished, while once flourishing estates were abandoned since there were no heirs to undertake their maintenance.

While the young, beautiful and wealthy did their best to enjoy life, albeit frantically, for most ordinary people the Twenties were a sad time, and the Thirties little better as the economic Depression left many without work. As this gradually lifted, the rise of Nazism in Germany brought the prospect of another war ever closer.

British society responded for the most part in a depressive mode, buckling down to the necessity of surviving as best it could. This mode was intensified with the outbreak of the 1939 - 45 conflict. There then developed a strong sense of a shared fate, the community pulling together and being mutually supportive. There was, inevitably, delinquent behaviour expressed in such ways as the black market economy. Many used it to ease the impoverished existence imposed by rationing and general shortages, but such naughtiness tended to ease the tensions of living under threat rather than seriously damaging the common wheal.

This essentially depressive mode of functioning continued for some years after the end of hostilities. As a country we were bankrupt, rationing gradually eased but continued until 1953, and there was little superfluity of anything. Life remained grey. However, there was hope, there was a great sense of relief at having survived, and attempts were made to inject some sense of jollity into the social scene, such as the 1951 Festival of Britain with its gaiety and promise for the future.

Short skirts and regression

Then something shifted in the Sixties. There had been a lot of babies born immediately after the menfolk returned home from war — a healthy response from a society which had felt its very survival under threat. This generation were now coming to adulthood. They had never known the austerities of their parents' lives; they had been indulged by those very parents who wanted something better for their children than they themselves had experienced. The contraceptive Pill had brought a sexual freedom never before known. The socialist Welfare State promised cradle-to-grave care. The world of these young adults was totally different from that of the previous generation, and they chose to divorce themselves from any sense of continuity with the past.

In many ways, the phenomena which began in the Swinging Sixties are typical of what happens in societies which have endured major wars.

War is shocking, traumatic — to society as a whole as well as to individuals. It generates intolerable anxiety, which fuels the need to fight while the conflict lasts, but lingers afterwards in the group.

The functioning of that group can become distorted, commonly by denial. The sense of relief encourages a turning away from the horrors of what has been happening. It has taken a century, and the final passing of those few who lived through the actual experience, for our society to turn around and face the appalling reality of 1914-18.

While the bereaved put their heads down and did what they could to re-construct their broken lives, others found their sadness intolerable. We had the Flapper age, when those young enough and wealthy enough had great fun. The Swinging Sixties was a similar phenomenon. In both instances, for those caught up in the social whirl there was a refusal to grow up, a reluctance to accept boundaries and responsibility, a regression into immature behaviour and an exploration of perversion.

For another more intellectual sub-group there was a retreat into schizoid intellectualism. Science and rational thinking became the fashion, with an under-valuing of the emotional aspects of life. Left brain thinking came to dominate over the Right brain perspective.

The slide towards perversion

These two modes could have counter-balanced each other in a more settled phase of society. However, what was missing were the concerned, functional moral values. People had had enough of these for too many difficult years. The slide towards perversion took hold with its erosion of boundaries, denial of difference, grandiose fantasies, and unrealistic expectations.

It took some years before the consequences became apparent. Then, what had been thought of as the basic pillars of society began to crumble.

- In Britain a number of Members of Parliament from the major political parties were arraigned for cheating on their expenses.

- It became apparent that the banks had been behaving with gross irresponsibility, and that the financial sector was out of control.

- It has been alleged that the Police Federation, disgruntled with their lot, framed a provocative member of parliament. He then resigned his ministerial post.

- The scandal of phone-hacking by the press led to the close-down of a long-established newspaper, and the prosecution of a number of journalists.

- A few cases of paedophilia, when investigated, revealed a disturbingly widespread problem — in the Roman Church, in children's care homes, among prominent citizens. Now we are dealing with the grooming of very young women for sexual exploitation by criminal rings.

- At the same time, the cost of housing puts home ownership out of the reach of many young people of child-rearing age, even those of the professional class. When they do struggle to achieve their own space by dint of both marital partners working, what happens to the children? Is this arrangement in the long-term social good?

I have described what I understand as the long-term reactions to war as a social trauma, having personally lived through a time of extraordinary change.

In the historical past, during such a lengthy period of uncertainty, those participating in the conflicts survived as best they could in an essentially pragmatic mode, while dipping for respite into the unbridled sensory behaviour of rape and pillage — hence the 'licentious soldiery' of repute.

Those largely untouched (as was possible when fighting was much more localised and small-scale than in later times) doggedly tried to continue the basic routine of life, as determined by the seasons and the needs of their livestock. If sensory indulgence was thin on the ground, a well-developed concerned/depressive mode was vital.

Three generations

A hundred years may seem to be a long time for a society to again achieve some level of normality after a period of destabilisation. I suspect that it is a typical time-scale. After three generations, those living through the initial trauma will have gone, and the memories of the events will have lost their power. It has taken this long for our society to face the awful reality and destruction of the 1914-18 war.

In England, after the upheaval of the 100 Years War, and the Wars of the Roses, it was not until the Tudor dynasty came to power that something like social stability was restored. If life remained brutal in some aspects, that was the norm in the Europe of that period. Meanwhile, the creative arts flourished, the court enjoyed its measure of hedonism, and if the politics became too uncomfortable it was still possible to retreat to the shires and lead a quiet existence, as did Anne Boleyn's elder sister Mary.

Further de-stabilisation occurred when Henry VIII, for his own personal reasons, retrieved the Anglican church from the Roman hegemony, thereby leaving a legacy of religious tensions which were played out down the subsequent years.

6. Sources of challenge

While war is a major destabilising factor for any society, there are others. It could even be argued that societies often go to war when they are already threatened by disintegration from other forces, in a desperate attempt to engender unity.

Epidemics

Throughout history disease has been a great killer. By AD 800 Europe's population was only half what it had been two centuries before, as a result of the Plague of Justinian, while between AD 1300 and 1400 the Black Death caused world population to fall from 450 million to under 375 million.[1] Following this mediaeval epidemic there were widespread and long term reverberations.

Today, while in the UK we seem to have weathered the worst of the HIV infection (whose virulence now appears to be declining), Aids has wreaked havoc in many communities in sub-Saharan Africa, and continues to do so. More recently we have the Ebola virus presenting a considerable threat in those areas affected.

---

[1] Both epidemics were probably caused by the bacterium *yersinia pestis*, now successfully treated using antibiotics.

Migration

Human beings have always been on the move from the time we wandered northwards out of Africa. Over millennia, we have come to inhabit all the corners of the globe that can sustain life. We have shown remarkable courage, stoicism and adaptability. We have survived, flourished and developed as a species, and exhibited impressive creativity in the process.

However, it is one thing to migrate into empty territory or areas where there are few other people; it is another to migrate into places which are already inhabited, possibly crowded, and have their own distinctive culture.

Recent years have seen a massive increase in migration, usually by people from poor countries to more wealthy ones, and frequently fleeing unsatisfactory and often dangerous conditions in their native land. While refugees may be initially tolerated and even welcomed, after a time the host community feels over-whelmed and threatened — by the sheer numbers as well as by any cultural differences.

Often with the best of intentions we have created, or rather allowed, some very difficult situations to develop in Europe.

Sheer numbers are part of the problem. What proportion of newcomers to native population is tolerable? Newcomers understandably tend to congregate together — but then ghettos develop, and the native locals begin to feel pushed out of their familiar streets and towns, and they resent it. Resentment is worse if the newcomers are willing to work for lower wages, as is often the case.

Differences of dress, of speech, of behaviour, become sources of aggravation. Religious differences become divisive. Colour of skin begins to matter. Paranoia all too easily sets in on both sides.

Politicians have been slow to recognise the problem, the depth and head of feelings that are around. In the UK it is now late in the day, and the formation of the UKIP Party has de-stabilised the essentially two-party parliamentary system of power that we have had for a long time. Politics has become unpredictable.

The UK has absorbed many immigrants at one time or an-other, and in time will undoubtedly integrate the current wave if numbers can be moderated. There was a massive in-flux of Ashkenazy Jews into 19th and 20th century England. For a while whole areas of London's East End became a *de facto* Jewish ghetto with shop signs typically in Yiddish.

Predictably, anti-semitism was a concern, and openly ex-pressed even as late as the 1930s, when Oswald Mosley led his Fascist marches through the streets. Latent anti-semitism enabled some of those in power to ignore and deny the infor-mation coming out of Nazi Germany about the fate of the Jews there.

After 1945 this was no longer an acceptable mind-set. Many Jews have now become Reformed and Liberal in their relig-ious practice so they no longer stand out sartorially from their neighbours. Their contribution to the common social life has been enormous and respected. Anti-semitism in the UK — as distinct from anti-Zionism — is nowadays mostly limited to a Muslim sub-group.

The Irish community could tell a similar tale. In the early 20th century, many came to the UK as labourers, some bringing their families with them. They were often treated with disdain, and even refused lodgings on account of being 'Paddies.' It is a long time since I last heard epithets of that kind used. The Irish no longer stand out from the crowd.

How long does it take for people to become assimilated? I suggest three generations at the very least. The first generation choose to come, albeit out of economic or political necessity. They want a new life, but still have ties to their homeland, and cling to their old familiar way of life. They bring their children up at home much as they themselves were brought up, with certain attitudes and assumptions which may be rather different from the values of their adopted country. The menfolk, because they are out in the workplace, tend to adapt more quickly to the different mores of their neighbours. Their womenfolk, particularly if there is a language barrier, can find it more difficult. Did they wish to make the transition in the first place?

The second generation are caught between two cultures, that of their family of origin and that of their new home. They carry the major burden of tension. Parental values may clash with those of their peer group at school, who may have greater freedom and different expectations. Adolescence, which always carries the seeds of rebellion, is a particularly challenging time when sexual behaviour become an issue.

It has become apparent that many of the current crop of jihadists are second generation immigrants. They do not properly belong anywhere; they do not know who they are, or what is their future role. Like all young people, they want to be of significance, to feel valued and respected; it is never easy for young men, and particularly so if you feel you are low in the social hierarchy. The natural idealism of the young makes them ripe for recruitment to a cause, ripe for radicalisation.

By the third generation, memories of the old country, the old culture, are fading within the immigrant families. There is more sense of belonging to the new. The grandchildren know little else. Integration is on its way — but it does take time. If the original immigrants had any idea of what lay in front of them, how many would still make the same choice?

Because of its history, the US has rituals which help the newcomers to feel part of the nation. It is only partially successful — they still have their ethnic ghettos, their racial tensions — but saluting the flag every morning in school is something everyone does, and it helps the newcomer to feel part of the whole. There is a tradition that one leaves behind one's old life in order to become an American. Their names may still reveal their origins, but the people themselves are often unaware of their names' significance. Something is lost in the process — a sense of one's roots — but the intent is that it encourages social cohesion between many diverse people.

Slavery

Slavery has a long history. All the ancient civilisations were based on it, including those Classical ones — the Greek and Roman — to whom we pay such respect.

We have indications that the Celts practised it. We know that the Vikings did; they plundered Ireland to carry off its population.

African tribes sold members of other tribes into slavery to the Arabs long before the white man set foot on African soil. When European traders arrived on the African coast to transport black people to America, they were met by African traders who had long been in the business, and had it well organised.[2] The white man did not go into the continent's interior to hunt for his supplies. He was just a new market for a long-established practice.

When the only available source of power was human muscle, one can understand why. It enabled a proportion of society to maintain a good standard of living, albeit at the expense of others. When over-shot watermills were first invented as a new source of power — at a time when Constantinople was the capital of the Roman Empire — there was some opposition to them from senior Roman dignitaries who suggested that they would undermine the institution of slavery. They were right!

One institution encapsulated a wide variety of experience. Slaves were treated differently in different cultures. In some, they could buy themselves out if they could find the wherewithal. In some, the children of slaves were free men, in others the condition was hereditary, in perpetuity. In some it was an aspect of the legal system — a punishment — when the condition could be imposed for a limited period of time. Sometimes people would sell themselves into slavery in order to pay off a debt that they could not service any other way. The 10th century laws of Hywel Dda in Wales which permitted this practice were particularly enlightened for their day.

---

[2] Arab traders bought three female slaves to every one male. For Europeans this ratio was almost exactly reversed.

We all have slaves who meet our needs and hopefully pander to our every whim. They are called mothers or nannies or ayahs and so on. Without them we would never survive our time of total dependency, our infancy. It is when this relationship is protracted beyond its appropriate time that it distorts what follows.

During our infancy we are doubly dependent; we are utterly dependent on others, and if we are fortunate we do not even realise the degree of our dependency. If the care we receive is so deficient that we come to realise our dependency prematurely, it creates a level of anxiety which is likely to persist as a permanent character trait.

When slavery is a settled social institution, it is not only damaging and degrading to the slaves, it also damages the masters. It encourages them to persist in childish characteristics, taking for granted and not acknowledging the support they receive. They are discouraged from developing their own skills in managing the outside world, with resulting impoverishment of ego-development and their own capacity to change and adapt.

They can only tolerate the cultural organisation of slavery by denying the reality — by not seeing the condition of their enslaved fellow human beings. Indeed they de-personalise them so that in their minds the others become things — to be exploited as needed and then discarded when no longer useful.

They cannot afford to develop those attitudes of compassion and caring which hopefully come with maturity. They cannot afford to without feeling deep discomfort and disquiet. A few do, of course, and some of them have come down in history, often in a religious context. Their insights have not necessarily been welcomed since they de-stabilise the status quo!

Slavery is inherently a de-stabilising factor in society since it creates an under-class who rightly feel exploited and de-humanised. If they are not so browbeaten that they feel nothing, they inevitably feel anger and resentment and envy. Sooner or later it explodes. The fact that such rebellion usually fails only leads to a tightening of controls and a deterioration of their conditions — until next time.

Their masters are further de-humanised in the process. Meanwhile, the tendency is for the rulers to become ever more effete and hedonistic in their life-styles. At some point the society comes under attack from outside, and collapses.

However, for the slave population lasting damage has been done. Families are initially torn apart; subsequent family structures and bonding are discouraged. What is left is a population of people who have no internalised model of normal family life on which to build.

I suspect that many of the difficulties in contemporary sub-Saharan Africa are the long-term results of slaving between tribes. It has left behind a level of paranoia which makes political cooperation and compromise very difficult. So much of the poverty there is unnecessary, and the result of political infighting and ineptitude. Trust is thin on the ground.

When the menfolk are the primary targets of enslavement, the women are left to cope as best they can, and in some communities there is a tradition of strong and enterprising women, who are lively entrepreneurs as well holding the families together. Admirable — but where does it leave the men? What role do they then have?[3]

Slavery in the USA is a recent episode in the history of the institution. If it is now viewed as shameful, it is to the credit of that culture that there were sufficient people with social consciences to oppose it and bring about its end. There are, though, those who would argue that its demise was in sight anyway for purely economic reasons.

However, it has left problems in its wake. Racism in that country has an ugly history, and although much has been done legally to stamp it out, it is far from dead. Speaking generally, the standard of living of black people is lower than that of the white citizens, their educational opportunities are poorer, there is a higher proportion of them in the prison population. The gross disruption of the family life of the African slaves inevitably created a lot of dysfunctional families, who in turn created emotionally damaged descendants.

The condition of African Americans is improving but it will take many generations for the damage to heal out. It has left a legacy of paranoia and a high incidence of violent crime in its wake. I am not suggesting that this is the only source of violent crime in the US, however. The initial treatment of the native Americans was brutally insensitive, and the settling of the land by force and gun culture has left its mark in the wider culture.

---

[3] Todd, Emmanuel. (1985) *The Explanation of Ideology*

Slaves of another kind

Today we all have slaves of a sort, the difference being that their work is done not by human strength but by sand power. The microelectronics revolution based on the silicon chip has revolutionised our society. Many of us have a higher standard of living, with more leisure than ever before, thanks to the many labour-saving devices at our elbow. They are powered by that non-human intelligence we call computers; and in the UK most of us have far more computers in residence than there are people — in our washing machines, dish-washers, microwave cookers, central heating boilers, mobile telephones, and cars. They are silent, unobtrusive, reliable and undemanding, and we can ignore them until they malfunction, which is surprisingly infrequent. Then we can replace them without a qualm of conscience.

Some things they cannot do; there are some situations where another human being is needed. We may then have to call on professional men or women, whom we pay handsomely; or they may be care assistants or domestic help in which case we pay them a pittance and under-value their input. These latter folk are the nearest we have to the slaves of former times, but even their situation is a great improvement on what was.

Is this situation in any way a threat to us as a society? I have suggested that the institution of slavery encourages a lurch in the direction of the Romantic/hedonistic modality, and we have indeed seen this in recent decades. There are many factors that have contributed to this, but it is perhaps something to watch.

7. The perils of progress

It is a paradox that many changes in society that are aimed at improving prosperity and life-style all too often bring with them their own challenges.

Technology

Developments in technology are often a response to changing social circumstances — an attempt to stabilise a community under threat — but in their turn they initiate further change. Their potency can be under-estimated.

Rapid technological innovation is a mixed blessing. The Industrial Revolution has brought an enviable standard of prosperity to the UK and Western world; living through it was a nightmare for many ordinary people. Rural poverty was no joke, but the conditions in the rapidly expanding towns were appalling — over-crowding, inadequate sanitation, dangerous working conditions.

Some concerned entrepreneurs looked to the welfare of their employees — the Quakers had a good record in this respect — but for others, intent on the business and its profitability at all costs, the needs of their workforce were ignored as far as possible. Children — often very young — were exploited; safety precautions thought an unnecessary luxury; there was no provision for industrial casualties. In a country which thought of itself as civilised, practice was often barbaric.

In due course the law caught up with practice, but as always it was slow. Banning small children from sweeping chimneys was suggested by Lord Shaftesbury in Parliament in the 1770s, (when six was considered the best age for a child to be apprenticed to this trade); but it was not until 1875 that a law was actually passed.

Trade unions were formed in the face of much opposition and hardship, but they performed a vital function for working men. If they subsequently came to be seen as a source of unhelpful rigidity and conservatism, it is hardly surprising given their roots.

Today we are in the midst of another technological revolution which has developed at an even faster rate than the earlier one based on mechanical and steam power. The electronic and communication revolution is changing our society at a prodigious rate, and we have yet to experience its ultimate effects. It has given us computers and mobile phones, ever more miniaturised, ever more complicated.

We now have more computers in our homes than there are people — in our washing machines, our central heating, our cars. It has given us instant access to our friends across the country and across the globe. It is estimated that 78% of phone users now do texting!

This revolution has undermined the power of the forces of law and order, and of the politicians. It is well-nigh impossible to keep anything secret — for good or ill. It encourages instant shopping, instant gratification. It exposes people to communications which could be exploitive, criminal, pornographic, misleading — and where it is difficult to check the reality. It leaves little space for quiet or contemplation. It is going to change our society.

Again, the law will follow to deal with the worst forms of misuse — albeit slowly as always. In the meantime, how do we protect and educate our young? How do we protect what is important to us?

A recent very different triumph of technology is fracking — the ability to drill sideways to tap the reserves of gas and oil trapped between layers of shale deep within the earth's crust and even beneath the sea.

Within 3-4 years, the USA has gone from being a major importer of oil into being self-sufficient in fuel. Meanwhile the price of oil has slumped from a high of nearly $160 a barrel down to under $60.

What is this going to do to the wealthy Arab Gulf States? What it is going to do to Russia, whose economic recovery after the collapse of the USSR has largely depended on exporting oil-derived gas? Their politics will change. Their relationships with the rest of the world will change. It will have its effect on the internal dynamics of these societies.

Technology and dependency

I am personally uneasy at being reliant on so much technology which I do not properly understand, despite having had a basic scientific education, and also having a personal mentor by my side who attempts to educate me further.

Such unthinking dependency is not good for people generally, though I am impressed by the flexibility many have shown in coming to terms with personal computing, texting etc. I am particularly impressed by the young who have grown up with these artefacts, and can switch with ease between different varieties of computers, for example.

I look back to a time when many men and boys spent much of their leisure time fettling their cars and motor-bikes; and they developed many skills as well as a close camaraderie in the process. Nowadays that is no longer possible, as cars have become so much more sophisticated that even the repair garages need to have their own computerised machines to help diagnose faults. The camaraderie has retreated to the interior of their workshops.

My current car is a much more sophisticated, comfortable, fast and reliable machine than the basic old banger that I first drove fifty years ago. However, something has been lost in the process, and if our society is currently short of engineers, I suspect there is a connection here somewhere.

Our ability to shop by inter-net and have the goods delivered by the next day feels like magic. The virtual relationships discovered on the inter-net, which may turn out to be quite other than they pretended, can make for disturbing experiences. The widespread acceptance of debt as a way of life — with frequently disastrous consequences — speaks to me of people who have lost touch with financial reality.

The inability to distinguish between virtual reality and external reality threatens our capacity to deal with real-life situations. It can inhibit our maturational development. It needs to be watched.

Education

Education can be a destabilising force. I note that with regret, being of the generation of young people who benefitted enormously from their educational opportunities. Post-1945, for the first time, it became possible for intelligent children from modest backgrounds to enter the grammar schools, and thence go on to university — all at public expense. It opened hitherto undreamed of possibilities of careers, of remuneration, of life-styles. It made for social mobility, for economic and geographical mobility. The class barriers began to crumble.

It is only in retrospect that one can see the price that was paid. Working-class parents lost their children, who became a different kind of people with different values and expectations. Children lost effective parents — their own were not able to give them appropriate advice about their new world. Parents could feel bereft and envious, and ambivalent about what they had sacrificed. Children could feel unsupported, misunderstood, resentful and, at worst, scornful.

The changes were only an exaggerated form of what frequently tends to happen between generations — but it was greater than anticipated. Some families coped with pride; others were disturbed and damaged by the process. Some university students dropped out of their courses, not because they lacked the necessary intelligence, but because they could not manage the tensions.

Above all, it weakened the extended family as younger members tended to move geographically from their place of origin. Since our culture is based on the nuclear family, the result is that there is all too little in the way of safety nets when times are hard. It is when the young begin to have their own small children, when the grandparents become old and unwell, that the price — the absence of family, the lack of a supportive community — becomes apparent.

Educational migrants

So many of us have become social migrants within our own country of origin; we do not properly belong anywhere. As time goes on, other ways of managing develop. We have nurseries, nursery schools, au pairs, day centres etc. They have their place and their virtues; but their roots do not run deep. Too many of us have become displaced people. It does not make for social stability.

If this is true in our country, the effects of education in developing countries can be equally mixed. Too many of the brightest and best go abroad for their higher education and never return. Our National Health Service is staffed by many people from abroad — to our advantage, but to the impoverishment of their countries of origin.

One of the most delightful and caring nurses I met during a brief hospital stay came from the Philippines. She had left behind three small children. They were cared for within her extended family, and she was earning money on their behalf at a level not possible at home. I was grateful to her. However, I did not feel comfortable about the situation — for her or for them.

Education is a powerful tool for social change. We have firm evidence that the surest way to reduce population growth is to educate the women. With more time and energy they then develop other interests, set up small businesses, compete with the menfolk, insist on having more of a say in public affairs. The Taliban may do its best to frustrate these changes where its rule runs. One feels it is bound to fail.

Ultimately an educated population is better able to manage its affairs, and the challenges that life brings. However, it is not an unmixed blessing; and the education on offer needs to be appropriate. Different communities have different needs.

Technological education is one thing; abstract science is another; philosophical and sociological theories are something else. The closer to people's actual lives, the more useful education is likely to be; the further removed, the more destabilising.

In the Sixties, in university Humanities departments of the UK, and under the influence of Post-Modernism, it was fashionable for teachers to explicitly challenge their students' belief systems and assumptions. Their expressed aim was to enable the students to think for themselves, freed from the weight of their past conditioning. It may have worked that way for some; for others it was a de-stabilising experience, leaving them bewildered and at sea.

In a group vulnerable if only because of age and biology, some sought relief in too much alcohol or recreational drugs. It was an attitude typical of a perverse society — the erosion of boundaries and the destruction of meaning — and contributed to a further slide in that direction. At the time it was notable that the students in the Departments of Engineering rarely got drawn into these fashionable social patterns!

8. A testing pace

Rate of change

Behind many of the factors tending to de-stabilise a society there is a single common factor — a rapid rate of change.

Some of us thrive on it; they enjoy the challenge, the stimulation, the sense of new and better things ahead. Others find it threatening. Those rearing young families need stability and predictability in order to fulfil their basic function. This is particularly true for the women, who are vulnerable when pregnant and while responsible for caring for their young.

At the other end of life, when one's physical and mental resources are declining, one has enough challenges to manage, and a stable environment is more conducive to contentment.

In the days when the average life expectancy was around forty, one could reasonably expect that the skills learned during the growing-up years would be sufficient to carry one through one's adult life (and earn the respect of the younger members of the tribe.) Nowadays that is far from true.

A certain level of stress can make for creativity and a sense of aliveness; too much can be overwhelming, for the individual and the community, bringing with it the threat of chaos and disintegration.

Politicians should beware their propensity for sweeping re-organisation. It may be counter-productive! They should beware also of their tendency to live at some remove from those they profess to serve. It is all too easy for them to become insulated from the stresses outside the political village.

Where next?

There are no quick fixes. It has taken us a long time to slide from the optimistic austerity and social concerns of the post-1945 Socialist government and the introduction of the Welfare State, to our current situation where the NHS feels to be on the verge of disintegration.

A recent commentator[1] suggested that the financial sector and the banks have developed a corrupt internal culture, and that it will take a long time for trust to be re-established. Trust has indeed become a casualty, and where is our corporate life without it!

We need to accept that the price of war is too high whichever way one views it as a human activity. We are still paying the price of the twentieth-century wars in social dysfunction, and the financial cost of keeping Trident while our police force is undergoing desperate cost-cutting makes no sense.

We have a problem with our young men which needs to be addressed in wide social terms. Many of them feel that they have no social function. Their womenfolk nowadays compete with them all too successfully; we can no longer send them off to fight; they have a lot of energy fuelled by high levels of testosterone. If many of them become depressed and suicidal, if

---

[1] Alex Brummer *The Week* 22nd November 2014

others wander off to become jihadists, we should not be surprised. Is there a possible solution in some form of community service comparable to the National Service of yesteryear?

I believe that the current epidemic of obesity epitomises our situation; it is, so to speak, a metaphor for much that is amiss in our society. People eat too much because the food that they do eat is lacking in essential nutrients. It has become over-processed and de-natured, so people eat ever more in a doomed attempt to compensate for the nutritional deficiencies.

We then find that we are spending a unduly large proportion of NHS funds treating patients with type 2 diabetes — a consequence of long-term malnutrition. In final desperation we resort to bariatric surgery. These measures are commendable, but they do not tackle the root cause.

We have no excuse for eating rubbish — for an inadequate diet. During the 1939-45 war, food was in short supply and monotonous — we had rationing of basic foodstuffs for many years. Nonetheless, the health of the general population was surprisingly good during that time.

Our current problem of obesity is self-imposed. However, it is not a moral issue, it is a failure of deep understanding and of education. We need more respect for our bodies, for the basic processes of life, for allowing time and thought for those fundamental activities which support it.

Resources squandered

We need to stop squandering our resources as if supplies are limitless. We squandered too many young men in 1914-18 and 1939-45; we squandered our North Sea oil by selling it off too cheaply; we have squandered our manufacturing base by allowing others to take it over. By our profligacy in use, we have squandered the great boon of antibiotics, and have left ourselves uncomfortably vulnerable to infections. We should beware of squandering the time interval of energy sufficiency that fracking can give us. Instead we should use that time and that income to invest in the long-term sustainable resources of wind and tidal power.

We need to understand that increasing bureaucracy and attempts at micro-management are inevitable reactions to the lack of internalised restraints in the populace. The fact that they do not work will not inhibit politicians and civil servants from trying to impose such bureaucratic centralism, out of anxiety and, sometimes, personal power seeking. It is a stopgap and inadequate response.

Above all we need a spiritual revival. There is a great hunger for spirituality at the same time as church attendance declines. An Evangelical Revival as of the early 19th century is not attractive, though fundamentalist groups have flourished in the United States as they are now doing within Islam.

We need a shared perspective which is congruent with our current scientific understanding of our world. We need to find a formulation which can unite those qualities which are at the heart of all the great religions — respect for our world, and compassion for those inhabiting it.

9. Which way the future

Freud stated that the sign of health was the ability to love and to work.

Work:

- provides livelihood,
- structures time,
- hopefully allows an outlet for, and stimulates, creativity,
- gives status,
- defines one's role in society.

Love is the basis of relationships

- within the family context,
- in face-to-face groups,
- in the wider society.

The innate human disposition seems to be to live in relatively small face-to-face groups. Once we operate in larger groups, social organisation becomes political, open to abuse, less meaningful to the individual. 'Socialisation' — the internalisation of standards acceptable to the wider society — becomes more imperative, but more difficult to achieve. How can we facilitate the individual's ability to identify with the wider society? The alternative is alienation, exploitation of social resources, criminality.

Our society needs to retreat from its present position. It needs to live more locally. It needs to value its communities where they still exist, and have not been destroyed by thoughtless 'development and improvement'. It needs to hang on to its village schools, its Post Offices, its small shopping areas, its local hospitals.

We need to encourage extended families to stay close, after a period of massive social and geographical dispersal. It has left vulnerable the young parents, the elderly, the less than fit.

We need to find a mechanism for socialising the young adult. University education does it for those who achieve it, though it is arguable whether it is appropriate for all those to whom it is offered.

I favour some kind of civilian equivalent of the former National Service. If handled appropriately, it could provide the young person with a mixed social group of contemporaries who might stay in contact after the experience had ended. [1]

- It could teach useful skills — there is plenty of community work currently not done.
- It would take individuals out of the stultifying, hopeless 'sink estates' in which they are trapped, and show them other possibilities.
- It is needed to break up the gang culture of our inner cities.

Globalisation is a disastrous fantasy. It denies the reality of cultural difference. It allows the unscrupulous to exploit the rest — as in the recent banking crisis.

---

[1] This happens among some university student groups.

The retreat from personal encounter — in the public libraries, in the banks — isolates us ever more. It is to be resisted. The profit motive should not be paramount in public services. Unbridled accountancy is destructive.

The internet is a mixed blessing. It allows us easy and rapid communication — wonderful! However, it is not a total substitute for face-to-face encounter. It does not provide the reality check of bodily gesture, smell, touch. It denies the reality of space and distance. It encourages us to live in a fantasy world — some of it malevolent. Perversion flourishes where there is no reality check.

Small scale societies

We need to look at those small scale societies which appear to work — Switzerland, Norway, Wales. Switzerland has solved the difficulties of weaving disparate ethnic and language groups into a cohesive whole. It has done this by keeping central bureaucracy to a minimum, and allowing the separate cantons maximum freedom. If the end-result is a somewhat over-disciplined mind-set, the Swiss clearly think it preferable to the petty warfare of the distant past.

Norway appears to have all the virtues of Scandinavia without the pervasive depression and alcoholism of the Swedes. They seem to enjoy life in spite of their climate and few natural resources. It is a notably egalitarian society, with a high standard of living maintained by high taxation, which appears to be well tolerated. There is a lot of evidence now that the more equal the society, the happier. The Norwegians seem to be a good example.

Wales has the virtues of a small, essentially face-to-face society. When a group of people meet together, almost their first activity is to search out their family and social connections! The clan organisation of old is still operative. It is as if everybody knows everybody in terms of being able to place them. The positive aspect of this is that the Welsh have been able to resist the onslaught of English culture in spite of six centuries of occupation.

The Welsh are still a different people with different attitudes and values. They have a feeling for the collective, for the co-operating group, which is very different from the competitive individualism of the English culture. Their variety of socialism is communitarian. Clan cohesion can lead, though, to something that from outside looks like corruption — as in other parts of the world.

They have a feeling for the family and for holding it together. They actually like children, and encourage their development to an impressive degree. The downside can be a certain lack of initiative derived from the need for family solidarity — perhaps inevitable if survival has depended on staying together. When they do fall out, they do so dramatically!

All three of these countries have a relatively low population density. Large conurbations are few. The landscape discourages urban sprawl. Mountains provide natural barriers. This may be relevant to their achievements.

Historically they have each had a powerful Protestant ethos, which has encouraged social responsibility while battling difficult external conditions.

None has grandiose global ambitions. They are not hampered by past experience of Empire. They can focus on what is needed now, and what is realistically possible. They are good places to live. What can they teach us?

There are straws in the wind. The demand for locally produced food is mounting rapidly. Farm shops are flourishing. The ever-rising cost of energy is having its impact. There is a move in the direction of less travelling, more internet contact within businesses. Government grants are on offer for roof insulation and solar panels. Small water-mills are being brought back into use, their excess power sold back to the grid on favourable terms. There are already three on the River Frome in Somerset.

The Tory leader David Cameron is looking, as of 2010, to return political power from the centre to local communities. He is also talking of the possibility of short, voluntary periods of community service for teenagers. Might this be a precursor for a more extended and developed scheme?

The Liberal-Democrats are promising to stop the building of more prisons, and to use other ways of dealing with minor offences. Is this an opportunity to further develop Restorative Justice? It is ridiculous that we have the highest prison population in Europe relative to our population — and it doesn't work! Of first offenders 90% re-offend.

Meanwhile, the banking industry, some of it government owned, continues to award its chief personnel grossly inflated salaries at the same time exhibiting visible signs of inefficiency and corruption. Yet the need for food banks is still with us.

The National Health Service is increasingly felt to be unsatisfactory, with the GP sector close to collapse. The teaching profession and the police force are both suffering from low morale, not least because they spend far too much of their time filling in forms.

The civil service has been allowed to have far too much say and influence in our public life — and that culture does not make for creativity, responsibility or personal human care. People are not robots. There are no neat algorithms for human behaviour. The law needs to define boundaries and limits; to restrain criminality and corruption. After that, too many rules and regulations deaden life, and infantilises the population. It won't do!

10. Betrayal

Betrayal is the cruellest of blows. It brings with it not only the loss of a relationship but also a loss of trust, loss of faith and loss of hope — and a sense of shame at having been made a fool of. It implodes one's normal and proper narcissistic defences.

It is an act of aggression — however covert — and it can provoke angry retaliation. In his play *Othello*, Shakespeare, with his characteristic insight, depicts a good man's disintegration following the false news of his wife's infidelity. Many a domestic tragedy stems from this source.

Social and political

There is such a thing as political betrayal. When Neville Chamberlain returned from a visit to Adolf Hitler in 1938, he thought he had negotiated 'peace in our time'. He was betrayed, his listeners felt betrayed, and he became an unfairly denigrated figure for many years.

When in 1958 the Right-wing General de Gaulle announced that 'he had heard them', the French colonists in Algeria — the *piednoirs* — assumed that he would fight their cause. His withdrawal of French troops and rapid settlement with the Islamist government made him a figure of hate. The embittered colons' sense of betrayal subsequently led to a number of attempted attacks upon his life.

There is also betrayal at a social level. The Highland Clearances of Scotland, the Potato Famine in 19th century Ireland, are tales of betrayal of subject peoples by the reigning colonial power. The treatment of the working poor in the heyday of the Industrial Revolution — driven by attitudes put forward by such as Malthus — was a betrayal by the government of the day of those they had a duty to protect.

The recent widespread scandals in the banking world have been experienced as a betrayal of trust, as has the evidence of corruption in the newspaper industry and also, it is alleged, in the Police Federation. Our political masters have been slow to take on board the depth of anger that is around in the general public. Social betrayal has been rampant for decades in our perverse society — the betrayal of our deepest biological needs.

Our young are, of all the animal kingdom, unusually immature and vulnerable when born. They need consistency and continuity of care which is most reliably given by those who love them. The fashion for young mothers to put their careers before their family, or the social conditions which propels the mother into that mode — the absent fathers, the cost of housing — have not been helpful.

A meaningless world

Too many children grow up feeling that the world does not make much sense, that no one really cares about them or is committed to their welfare, that they have to look out for themselves and snatch such satisfactions as are available. And we wonder why we have a drug problem, youthful binge drinking, a high rate of teenage pregnancies, and a lot of disaffected, intransigent, often depressed, young adults!

Sexuality is fundamental to our identity. For the woman, in earlier times, sexual activity usually meant pregnancy, a long-term commitment to child-rearing, and the need for a partner and others to help provide the conditions necessary for that task. The man's self-esteem was closely tied up with his ability to sire children, but also to his capacity to provide adequately for them. At its best, a good sexual relationship between the partners acted to cement that relationship.

In many ways we are not so very different from other animals. My garden attracts many birds, and blackbirds in particular tend to nest with us. It is interesting to watch the complete biological drama enacted each summer — the ritual courting, the different behaviour of cock and hen, the anxiety to find nest material and foodstuff, the fatigue of the parent with young to feed, the watchful care over the fledgling, the juvenile taking wing.

A good sexual relationship is a great gift. It can take us to depths of feeling we did not know we had. It can delight and sharpen our senses, invigorate our well-being, stimulate our creativity, and make our life feel worth living. It also contains the seeds of our deepest despair if it goes wrong. The poets throughout the ages pay testament to all this. We are fortunate to live in an age when adequate contraception has removed so much of the anxiety, and repressive attempts at social control, from sexual activity.

However, by trivialising sex, by commercialising it, by allowing it to become casual and superficial in meaning, we have betrayed something profound in our humanity. We have allowed the young — and the not-so-young — to squander something of great value, to renege on its potential deep meaning.

Some use it in an attempt to get the love they missed out on in childhood. Others get caught up in behavioural fashions and allow themselves to be exploited. It looks like freedom; it limits their development as human beings; it results in too many single parents, and a repeat of the cycle of deprivation. It is immensely sad.

Old and neglected

We are betraying our elderly. True, we have rather a lot of them relative to the working population. Care workers are in short supply, poorly paid and inadequately trained; and caring for the demented is not easy. One can understand, if not excuse, some of the behaviour that has come to light in residential homes.

What is totally unacceptable is the appalling neglect that has been found in NHS hospitals among those admitted as sick. It has revealed a failure of proper care and concern amongst people who have lost focus on the what their job is all about. The attempts to deny and cover up the failings simply emphasise the depths of the betrayal. It is failure at a professional level; it is a failure of basic human decency.

Ultimately, I suspect that how we care for the dependent and vulnerable depends on how we ourselves were cared for when we too were dependent and vulnerable. Are we rearing people who simply have no internalised model of how to do it?

Are we becoming so addicted to our technology as the solution of all problems that we robotise our very concept of people? Nurses are increasingly trained to be accomplished medical technicians, and their professional status has risen accordingly. Sadly, in the process, too many seem to have forgotten how to nurse. The basic needs of the human being who is the patient — to be fed and watered, to be kept clean and comfortable, to be reassured and feel cared for — these are being ignored. Such practice is a betrayal of our humanity.

A recent edition of the British Medical Journal [1] has an article which bemoans the effect of the computer on general practice, written by someone who had been an early and enthusiastic adopter. David Loxterkamp writes:

'It is reported that physicians spend, on average, 11 minutes with their patients and listen to their chief complaint for only 22 seconds before taking control of the interview.'

He goes on to suggest that what patients need is:

'reassurance, common sense advice, coordination of community resources, and knowledge of their family values. This was once our vital function, but no longer. We now see a greater value in access and efficiency than continuity of care.'

'Patients are not (only) data fields for the doctor to harvest, objects to be imaged, or problems to be solved. They are also our neighbours asking for help, using posture, gait, gesture, and facial expression to indicate where and how to proceed,

---

[1] Loxterkamp, David (2013) *BMJ* vol. 347.
    (2013) *What Matters in Medicine* University of
    Michigan Press.

Let's first acknowledge them beneath their symptom complex and accept the story of their illness in their own words. This takes time — face time, time looking into their faces instead of a clock or computer or a hundred other distractions that cloud our exam rooms.

Lastly, let's ask our patients if their concerns have been heard, our findings explained, their needs addressed.'

What a relief to find one's own frustrating experience so accurately mirrored!

A brain of two halves

Iain McGilchrist in his seminal book *The Master & His Emissary*[2] develops the idea that the Left-hemisphere functioning of our brain — the rational, reductionist, objective bit — has come to dominate our culture at the expense of the Right-hemisphere functions — those concerned with nuanced feeling, imagination and meaning.

He comments that the financial crash of 2008 was fuelled by the belief that human behaviour can be confidently predicted by algorithms — but goes on to say that we not only do not know, but can never know, enough to make this kind of prediction valid.

He points to the mass of petty legislation, and the obsession with accountability and audit in all walks of life, which is designed to fill the vacuum left by untrustworthiness, but which in practice further erodes trust. He cites the bureaucracy and micro-management which stifles originality in research and

---

2 McGilchrist, Iain (2009) *The Master & His Emissary* Yale University Press.

ensures mediocrity; the managerial culture which is destroying professionalism in medicine; and the neglect of practical hands-on, embodied experience and common sense that turns nurses and policemen into office-based paper pushers.

Robert MacFarlane[3] has an interesting perspective on maps. The development of cartography has enabled us to map the world in such a way that we can now locate ourselves with accuracy almost everywhere. However, he contrasts this with the maps of old which told a tale, which gave us a glimpse of what the landscape meant to those who travelled it, and in doing so told us so much about their thinking and their culture. An interesting example is the Mappa Mundi now housed in Hereford cathedral.

He also reminds us of those intuitive, idiosyncratic maps developed by people living and working in an unstable landscape. The Inuit have an understanding of cloud formations which allows them to know the depth and quality of ice under their feet. Men who fish for their livelihood develop an internal map of the sea-bed over which they work. He does not denigrate the grid map. It is just a different way of relating to the landscape.

Science has given us so much, has so enormously improved the standard of living for so many of us, has so widened our understanding of the world that it seems churlish to offer criticism. Yet the scientific method is a development of Left-brain thinking. What science offers us is not, as so often thought 'The Truth', but just a series of models of our world

---

3 MacFarlane, Robert (2008) *The Wild Places* Granta.

which work well-enough. When the models no longer work, we develop a new theory!

However, science does so by simplifying. It simplifies the language it communicates in, it simplifies the concepts it uses, it strips down, reduces, in order to make difficult thinking manageable.

That is fine as long as one recognises and remembers what is happening. The danger is that in simplifying, one strips out much meaning. If we lose sight of that, if we come to believe that the scientific world is the whole of the real world, we are deluding ourselves — and we are betraying our humanity.

The virtue of scientific stories are that they are continually being added to and amended as research reveals their limitations. The danger inherent in political fantasies is that they can become idealised and set in stone. This is even more true of religious stories. Both can come to limit and distort the lives of their adherents — another form of betrayal.

How we conduct ourselves

The careful observer can tell much about an individual by noting the posture and speech mannerisms, the clothes, the acquired possessions. Similarly, a dominant political group will reveal its hidden fantasies.

Remember the robot-like goose-stepping of Hitler's troops — and where that led? The Soviet army adopted a similar marching style during a period of history when their country was going through a crisis of child mortality. Emmanuel Todd, in

1976, prophesied[4] that a country that could not keep its children alive, would become a failing state. In its last days, the Soviet Union is reported as spending 27% of its Gross National Product on its military whilst infant mortality was rising. The formal acceptance of the Soviet Union's final disintegration came in 1991. The bleak architectural style favoured by the then Communist regimes did not suggest much sensitivity to the population's basic humanity.

Pyongyang, the North Korean capital city, has a 'Fine Art' gallery, as many capitals have. However this one contains only pictures of the three Great Leaders — the current president, his father and his grandfather. The country possesses nuclear weapons, but the population lives at starvation level, partly on food aid from the South. All such regimes betray their people.

I sense an uncomfortable loss of trust in the powers-that-be in our society as the decline in standards of public behaviour becomes ever more apparent. The political spectrum is changing as the long-established two-party system loses its grip. Both Scotland and Wales appear to be moving towards independence from Great Britain. Ultimately, betrayal has its consequences. Beware the revenge!

---

4 Todd, E. (1976) *The Final Fall* Karz (New York, USA)

11. A new politics

It is May, 2010 and New Labour has gone. For Gordon Brown, a flawed but decent man, a personal tragedy; but it needed to happen.

At the heart of socialism as a political theory is the desire to control everything from the centre. Socialism is defined here as a theory or system of social organisation that advocates the vesting of the ownership and control of the means of production and distribution, of wealth — capital, land, etc. — in the community as a whole.[1]

The basic underlying assumption is the one proposed by the philosopher Locke — that people are born as tabula rasa — and can be made into any shape by appropriate external circumstances. The 'New Soviet Man' was heir to this belief; it drove the French Revolution — and the American one! It has long had its day.

Another underlying assumption — that of equality — is obvious nonsense unless interpreted in a poetic or religious sense. In politico-social terms, it is a defence against envy.

It doesn't work. It cannot work. The systems are too complex to be micro-managed, and the attempt to do so leads to pro-

---

1 The socialism of Wales and Scotland is more communitarian than in England and, I sense, a remnant of the clan structure that still lingers in the Celtic fringes.

gressive economic failure, the suffocation of initiative, and the infantilisation of the populace.

What many people think of when they term themselves socialists — a concern for the social fabric — is closer to 19th century Liberalism.

The role of government

People are formed by the subtle and complex interaction between their innate endowment and the circumstances of their lives. We are all different. We each have inborn potential and talents; we each have a specific life-experience; we each have something unique to contribute.

The role of government is to facilitate, as best it can, the potential of its citizens, recognising that ultimately its people are the only wealth it can call on.

This requires as much liberty as possible within a framework of law. It requires a recognition that the earliest years of life are formative to a degree impossible to exaggerate; that subsequent interventions are relatively inefficient and costly. It requires a radical re-think of perspective and of priorities.

The ideals of socialism are admirable. The process has not worked because the basic unconscious assumptions have been faulty. What now?

12. A new morality

An ordinary morning. The media is buzzing with the Home Secretary's announcement about paedophilia in high places. Westminster, the civil service and the judiciary are all under investigation for activities that go back several decades. There is the suspicion that the Metropolitan Police Force has managed to 'lose' some dossiers forwarded from the Home Office.

Coming on the heels of the Leveson enquiry and the subsequent trials related to phone-hacking, the still-smarting unprofessional and exploitive activities of the major banks in recent years, the allegation of corruption in the Police Federation which resulted in unjustly framing an M.P., the erstwhile scandals of M.P.'s. expenses and cash-for-questions, it begins to feel as if all the structures which hold our society together are crumbling.

Over breakfast we speculate on what effect this most recent furore will have on the Scottish move towards Independence, and on the next general election.

The telephone rings — a cold call. A man with a sing-song accent tells us his records show that our *Windows* computer operating system is faulty. He tells us how to check the computer for the fault, and then offers to sort it for us for a certain fee.

This is a scam well known to my computer-savvy husband who has no intention of colluding with it. It is just a way of extorting money from the naive and inexperienced. Since the computers we have do not use *Windows* software, it was a particularly ill-judged attempt at theft.

However, one is left wondering how many people fall for it. Many of us are only just computer literate and easily gulled.

We are travelling towards our holiday destination up a long hill with some dangerous bends ahead. The speed limit is 50 m.p.h. for good reason. Most traffic respects the limit but a number of vehicles zoom past, leaving us gently plodding behind. The accident rate on this stretch of road is notoriously high. Fortunately, today we have a clear run.

All this before midday! I mutter to my companion — we surely do need a new morality. Many share my sentiment — but where can it come from? And on what basis?

The new morality

Historically, the Christian Church has spent much effort trying to coerce people into behaving better. I am not convinced that that is what religion is all about, but one can see that the Church did indeed have a moderating influence on the brutal cultural norms of earlier times.

Nowadays, only a minority of the population claim to be Christian. Many are alienated from all formal religion, and we have another sizeable minority who adhere to other faiths with different takes on matters of morality. It does not make for social cohesion.

Any new moral stance must be based on our current understanding of the world. It must encompass our existing scientific perspective. The Ten Commandants — Judaic and pre-Christian — no longer seem appropriate or adequate.

Among my many *objets trouvé* is a wooden carving of the Hindu god Shiva, such as one might find in many Hindu temples. With him is his (much smaller) consort Padma, a large snake — and perched on the snake a butterfly. In Hindu cosmology Shiva is the God of destruction — a necessary part of the cycle of ongoing creation. The snake represents Time, and the butterfly this immediate Moment of Time.

Those scientists interested in the theory of Chaos talk about 'the butterfly effect'. They suggest, by illustration of how the process of Chaos develops, that the fluttering of a butterfly's wings can set in motion a long series of related happenings which can ultimately develop into a typhoon. In other words, small apparently insignificant events can lead to momentous conclusions.

Typically our weather systems are chaotic. It has needed the development of massive computing power to give us the capacity for forecasting that we now have — and even so it is only accurate over a short period of time.

It can be argued that the development of a small child is a chaotic process in that very minor experiences (in adult terms) during the vulnerable early years can have a major impact on that child's future responses to life.

Parents will sometimes comment on how different their several children are, since 'we brought them up in exactly the same way.' This statement ignores several issues. Firstly, it takes no account of the different genetic package each of us brings into the world and which, by current understanding, accounts for approximately half of our individual characteristics.

Secondly, in terms of the infant's experience, there is no way the minutiae of care can ever be replicated for two siblings. A first child has Mother to itself; subsequent babies have to share her. Parents too are changed by the very experience of having a child, quite apart from developments in the rest of their lives. Life moves on, and any difference will be reflected in the detailed pattern of child nurture.

This is a paradigm of our ordinary day-to-day lives, did we but know it. Small events, whether good or bad, affect how we react subsequently, often at an unconscious level.

We meet briefly with a certain person; it is a positive interchange. Subsequently we meet someone similar, or in a similar situation, and we are more likely to react positively to them. Conversely, if we have a bruising encounter, next time we are in a similar situation or the stranger resembles the first aggressor, we are likely to be more defensive than is appropriate.

These apparently trivial encounters can subtly influence major decisions in our lives — about who we decide to trust, who to ignore, who to appoint to a certain job, and about how we first react in a strange group, thereby setting the tone of our future history in that group.

A trivial encounter

I recall as a young woman attending a meeting of a university wives' club. As a newcomer I was anxious to make friends with those of my own age, and espied a likely group that I might join. However, I happened to be sitting next to an older, rather depressed-seeming woman who engaged me in conversation in a way that pinned me to my chair. With some reluctance I let go of my own agenda, and stayed talking with her about her recent move to the area, about her family, and how alien she was finding the different culture hereabouts.

She subsequently became a good friend. A long-standing Quaker, she supported me in my spiritual quest, and encouraged me to become a voluntary Marriage Guidance counsellor. This latter experience was invaluable in paving the way for my later professional career.

 Although in time we left the area, on our return visits I was always sure of a warm welcome from her, and we remained in touch until her death. I owe her a great deal. This is the stuff of ordinary life. That does not make it insignificant.

There is a general principle here — that all our actions and words have their impact and to a degree we can never know. This applies to both the good and the bad that we do. All the time, we act in a way that is potentially creative, potentially destructive; that subtly shifts the future direction of events.

I am not suggesting that we abandon spontaneity, or that we should go around as if treading on eggshells. Honesty of emotional response is essential, and sometimes this involves confrontation and the speaking of uncomfortable truths. However, even such difficult matters can be handled in more than one way. We could all improve those skills which allow communication without stirring excessive aggression or inflicting unnecessary hurt.

What I am suggesting is a perspective that might provide a framework for thinking about our behaviour and its potential consequences. Moreover, it is a perspective that is capable of being integrated with such religious belief — or none — that we already have. It offers a morality that can be integrated with our scientific understanding of how the world works.

In a very real, concrete sense we are all the time subtly creating the world in which we live. If we could become more acutely aware of that, it would change us; it would change our relationships; it might even change our politics!

Finally a quotation[1]: 'God, who created all things in the beginning, is himself created by all things in the end.'

---

1 Olaf Stapledon

13. Credo

I am aware that, as I write, I make certain basic assumptions which underlie my personal perspective on the world and on our society. Perhaps I should spell them out.

What do we all have in common?

- We are human animals, and we share the basic biology of the human animal.
- We are sexual beings; we are aggressive in defending our territory; our young are very slow to develop to adulthood and need a long period of dependent nurturing.

  Many religions have gone off the rails by trying to deny these two realities — by retreating into 'other-worldliness'; by splitting the material world (bad) from the spiritual world (good); by attempting to suppress what is irrepressible by a denial of incarnation. These attempts to deny how things actually are distort people's lives, and ultimately break down.

- We are social animals. We are evolved to live in family groups, and in larger but still essentially face-to face groups. When the size of group grows beyond this, power struggles develop — and conflict — and politics.
- We have an innate need to make sense of our experience, and of the world we inhabit. If we cannot, we experience

existential anxiety which rapidly becomes unbearable. The threat is of chaos and a sense of disintegration. If we cannot make obvious sense, we make up stories to explain matters to ourselves. Any story is better than none.

- We are born with an innate religious sense. By religious, I mean a sense of something greater than ourselves, which holds our world together and upon which we are dependent. This may evoke a desire for greater closeness, greater comprehension, awe, fear, comfort, love.

These factors are the basis of the world's many religions. The stories people make up vary with time, place, culture, sophistication. They are all attempts to comprehend the incomprehensible. They are all inadequate. Ultimately it is beyond our comprehension.

Finding a pearl

From time to time there are a few remarkable people who see the world as it is. They have an intuitive understanding and experience of the numinous which illuminates their lives. It is 'the pearl of great price'. It is beyond words.

They attempt to communicate their understanding to others, but the words are always inadequate. They can only ever be symbolic, poetic, allusive. Unfortunately the words are all too often taken by their associates as expressing concrete reality.

Stories are created, rituals developed, patterns and organisations set up, on the basis of an inadequate comprehension. A religion is formed. It is comforting, it is illuminating; it is the best the group can manage.

The trouble comes when they come to think that they have *The Truth* and the whole truth, and that everyone else is wrong. Sadly, they cling to this conviction because their religion gives them comfort. It protects them from the existential anxiety which is so unbearable. They cannot afford to have it challenged.

The only way out of this dilemma, and the tensions arising from the clash of religious ideologies, is to face the fact that none of us can know the whole truth. It is beyond us; it is mind-blowing. Our brains are not adequate to grasp it. We have to learn to bear that anxiety.

We need to respect each other's attempts to struggle with ultimate reality and perhaps learn from those attempts. They were the best people could do at the time.

I believe that we live in a world that is in the process of creation, and that we are a part of that process. We each have a part to play in it. We can only make our contribution by being who we are to our fullest potential. We cannot be other than ourselves. We should not live to satisfy others' models and expectations, and it is blasphemous — and a waste of energy — to try.

By offering ourselves up to that process, we may find ourselves in strange places, doing unlikely things. It takes a kind of courage. 'It is a terrible thing to fall into the hands of the living God!'[1] It is our only salvation.

---

1 *The Bible* Hebrews, Chapter 10, Verse 13

14. Mysticism

What is mysticism but the transitory perception of Ultimate Reality — the breakthrough of the Eternal into our three-dimensional, time-ordered world? At such times we make contact with the source of life, we touch the fringes of heaven.

I can only talk about my own experiences. They came thick and fast when I was an adolescent and young adult. Listening to music was powerful, as was contact with the natural world — the landscape, mountains, the open skies. Later came a sexual relationship, nursing my babies. At such times the world was in tune, a good place, a whole, and myself as part of that whole. This was in such marked contrast to my frequent mood of unhappiness, struggle and depression. Those times carried me through. Without them I am not sure I would have survived.

It was only in my thirties that I came to make some connection with 'spirituality', and realised that these kind of experiences were shared by others, both present and past. It rarely felt safe to talk about them, but I did come to feel that within the Quaker context they would be understood.

Over the years, these episodes gradually diminished in frequency though still tending to recur at times of stress. Now in old age, I feel I rarely need them as once I did. They have gradually been replaced by a gentler, more continual sense of the world as God's ongoing creation. Like Brother Lawrence, I feel I can make contact with God just as well at the kitchen sink as anywhere else.

Nevertheless, the shared experience of the Quaker Meeting for Worship almost always touches me at that deep level, and it remains powerfully moving, and rather exhausting!

Did these experiences change me? They did not turn me into a saint; but they did enable me to change slowly from a tense, shy and rather withdrawn young woman into a reasonably sanguine and sociable normal adult. Only those who have grown up feeling 'odd' know what an achievement it is to feel 'normal'!

They did not send me out into the world to do great things, but helped me stay at home and attend to those matters that were under my nose and that only I could do, in spite of my frequent disinclination, boredom and frustration. I learned that creating anything of value is largely composed of such times of 'blood, toil, tears and sweat'[1]; and that it is out of them comes satisfaction and joy and a sense of achievement.

Subsequently it gave me the courage to return to my professional training and qualify as a psychotherapist. As such, I put to good use the insights my personal struggles had given me, and I was able to help some other people in their struggles towards growth and maturity.

I have come to accept the findings of the Alister Hardy Trust which suggests that these experiences of the numinous are universal in one form or another. Since we come out of eternity and finally return to it, is it surprising that we all have

---

[1] Winston Churchill

glimpses of it from time to time? Most of us don't talk about it because in our culture it is often suspect, even within the Christian church. It isn't done! And anyway we have no words. It is essentially an experience beyond words, though we may make the attempt to communicate.

The question remains for me as to why these experiences are more frequent, more available to some people than to others. It is as if for some, at certain times, the boundaries between this world and eternity become thinner, and there is a breakthrough. Wordsworth talked of heaven being around us in our infancy, and I have known a few people who had a powerful sense of God's love in their childhood. For some it occurs at the high points in their life, for others it comes at times of stress, of illness or bereavement.

Religion and psychosis

There seems to be some link between religious experience and a tendency to psychosis. A few undergo a temporary psychotic episode which they can subsequently integrate and experience as creative, while others go over the edge into madness.

There is a well-documented correlation between religious experience and epilepsy, implicating a particular area of the brain — Paul of Tarsus being a famous example.

There is a long tradition among the religious of many faiths of fasting in an attempt to attain a sense of God's presence, suggesting that certain physiological changes facilitate it. Since we are incarnate beings, it is hardly surprising if there are physiological accompaniments to these particular intense experiences, as to any others. Such correlations seem to me to be interesting but irrelevant to the meaning and significance they have.

Certainly a too rigid clinging to the external material world, a habit of concrete thinking, appears to have a negative correlation. Perhaps one has to be able to let go of the 'certainties' in order to allow the 'unknown' to enter. Is this only possible if one has had the experience as an infant of falling apart, and then finding oneself contained and upheld by the everlasting arms? If the human arms have not been there to rescue us from psychic disintegration, perhaps it is difficult, subsequently, to feel safe enough to let go.

Am I a Christian? I do not know. In the company of some professing Christians I feel comfortable and at home; with others I feel totally alien. The traditions of ritual and doctrine have little attraction or meaning for me, though I can find them intellectually interesting. I can appreciate that they perform a function in encoding the ongoing experience of the Church down the centuries so that it does not get lost, and remains available to those who seek.

The exhortation and moralising of some groups I find positively off-putting, but I firmly believe with William Penn that 'true religion don't turn men out if the world but enables them to live more fully in it and excites their endeavors to mend it.'[2]

There are many paths up the mountain: we each have to find the way that is right for us. I am grateful for what I have been given, and for having found some good companions on the journey.

---

[2] William Penn

15. Science and religion

I recall a time when 'Science' was the intellectual fashion. It promised us a clear-cut, hard-edged world, which made sense and relieved our existential anxiety. If there were still things to be discovered, things we could not yet understand, that would be remedied by time. We could maintain the belief that we, the human race, could ultimately know everything worth knowing, would one day be in control.

Religion was for wimps — for the superstitious and ill-educated. Religion was full of impossible happenings, tiresome people and tedious injunctions. We no longer had need of it. Science had made it irrelevant — a view still shared by some.

Then came the scientific developments of Quantum Physics and the Theory of Relativity. At the cutting edge of atomic research, the smallest particles of matter were discovered to be no longer the smallest but composed of even smaller ones, and these too could be split into ever smaller. Sometimes they behaved like billiard balls, but sometimes they behaved like waves — which were they? Sometimes they appeared out of nothing, which the philosophers had always said was impossible, and then they disappeared back into nothingness. Moreover, even when in existence, it seemed impossible to locate them exactly. Heisenberg proposed his Uncertainty Principle which in effect suggested we gave up the hopeless attempt. Now the physicists are talking about the fundamental particles as 'strings'!

Meanwhile, the science of Astronomy made us aware of the vast aeons of time and space in the universe; of the utter improbability that our small planet should have just those narrow conditions that has allowed the emergence of life, and the development of its myriad manifestations. We may be unique. If not we shall probably never know, since the terrifying, awesome vastness 'out there' precludes the likelihood of any communication with extra-terrestrials, even if they exist. Are we then just an insignificant speck of dust in a cold world, or are we singular, unique. If the latter, how then do we value our earthly home?

The erstwhile image of our clear-cut hard-edged world began to crumble around the margins. What we had left was less a photograph, more an Impressionist painting.

The determinedly unpredictable

Then came the Theory of Chaos. Chaos is the science of surprises, of the nonlinear and the unpredictable. It teaches us to expect the unexpected. While most traditional science deals with supposedly predictable phenomena like gravity, electricity, or chemical reactions, Chaos Theory deals with nonlinear things that are effectively impossible to predict or control, like turbulence, weather, the stock market, or our brain states.

These phenomena are often described by fractal mathematics, which capture the infinite complexity of nature. Many natural objects exhibit fractal properties, including landscapes, clouds, trees and rivers, and many of the systems in which we live exhibit complex, chaotic behaviour.

Chaos theory suggests that because we can never know all the initial conditions of a complex system in sufficient, in reality near perfect, detail we cannot hope to predict its ultimate fate. Small changes in the initial conditions lead to drastic changes in the end-results — a phenomenon we have come to know as 'the butterfly effect'. Our lives are an ongoing demonstration of this principle. Trivial events can ultimately lead to momentous changes.

Then — to add insult to injury — came the Theory of Complexity, which suggests that the elements of a complex system can spontaneously inter-act and self-organise until the system itself is changed into something quite different. The mind boggles! The fantasy of total understanding, total control has been exploded.

Science no longer performs its function of relieving our existential anxiety. As biologist, Marxist and atheist J.B.S. Haldane once remarked, 'The world is not only queerer than we know, it is queerer than we can know'. At the same time, recognising the chaotic, fractal nature of our world can give us new insight, power, and wisdom — if we can get our heads around it.

What now of religion? There is currently a widespread spiritual hunger at the same time that regular church attendance has dwindled.

Some have returned to religion in its well-structured fundamentalist forms. Christianity has its evangelical wing, offering reassuring unquestionable truths. Creationists have a powerful lobby in the USA. Islam has erupted painfully with its own brand of fundamentalism. Behind these manifestations is fear — fear of living in a world which does not make sense, which feels unmanageable, in which one feels all too vulnerable. The threat is of personal and social disintegration. It can feel like impending madness.

The prescription of anti-depressant drugs has quadrupled in the years since 1994 according to the British Medical Journal. Meanwhile it seems that the war against illegal drugs has had no noticeable impact on the widespread indulgence in 'recreational' drugs.

Where are Quakers in all this?

We are a very mixed bunch — and always were! We squabble in our journals — very politely — about the words we use. Can both theists and non-theists really be Quakers?

In the gathered Meeting for Worship we come together in an experience which is beyond words, in which we feel held, contained, aware of some power beyond ourselves, in touch with the creativity of the universe.

Afterwards, as we chat over our coffee, we revert to being our ordinary selves, but with the strength to do what needs to be done in our personal world, in the outside world, in our shared Quaker activities. At some deep level we have recognised one another, and our role in a wider enterprise.

We also recognise that the experience we have shared is something that has been experienced by others in different times and in different places. We recall Julian of Norwich (d.1416) saying, 'All shall be well, and all shall be well. and all manner of things shall be well.' We recognise it in the writings of Meister Eckhart (d. 1328); in those of the Sufi poets Ibn al-Arabi (b. 1165) and Jelaluddin Rumi (13th century); in the mystics down the ages.

It is an extra-ordinary, incommunicable, powerful experience. It offers us no certainties, no safety, except that of being part of an ongoing, inexorable process. We accept that we cannot be certain, cannot 'know' in any ordinary sense. What we have is a deeper level of understanding — of that which fuels our incarnate world, an experience of something in which we are embedded, on which we are utterly dependent, a power beyond our grasp, yet immediate and all-embracing.

We can only be faithful to that experience. It is what will carry us through — the only thing that *can* carry us through — a Faith for our time.

16. A critique of Christianity

Christianity — in its conventional institutional forms — is an inadequate religion for our time[1]. It fails in two significant areas. It is patriarchal in perspective; and it has a long history of negativity towards sexuality. Neither are currently acceptable in our culture.

This is not a rejection of the founding figure, Jesus of Nazareth, or of his life and insights insofar as we know them. He remains an intriguing, charismatic personality and an inspirational beacon of light. It is rather a comment on those who followed; who developed a cult and then a church, with its concomitant structures and hierarchies, and which inevitably bore the imprint of their own personalities and times.

It wasn't inevitable that Christianity became patriarchal. The evidence is that Jesus had a number of women closely involved with him. We are re-discovering that in the early years of the Church women played a significant and active role. While Judaism, the cradle of this new religion, had and still has well-defined gender roles, women are as powerful in their own sphere as are the men in theirs.

---

[1] A ludicrously sweeping statement about a very successful religion which, according to UNESCO statistics, has spawned 33,380 denominations! Nevertheless, I believe the comment is valid for our current society, where church attendance has been in steady decline for a long time, even though there are many signs of a widespread spiritual hunger.

However, when Constantine decreed that Christianity was to be the new imperial religion, it inevitably began to adapt to the Roman culture, and Athanasius was deputed to suppress those documents and attitudes which did not accord with its new status. Roman culture was essentially militaristic, and that mind-set contaminated the young Church.

Where Jesus talked of God as Father — a compassionate and forgiving father — God increasingly became to be seen as King who laid down rules and regulations to be obeyed.

The female element crept in by the back door in the form of the Virgin Mary, but she was kept firmly in her place on a pedestal, and far above mere human women. The Holy Ghost is referred to as 'she' in all early Greek documents, but not in the Western tradition, where all three personages of the Trinity are male.

Female saints had to be recognised, but they tended to be minor figures compared to their male equivalents. A few women in the mediaeval church became powerful figures — Hildegarde of Bingen, St. Hilda of Whitby — but they usually came from powerful aristocratic families which gave them status in their own right. Even so, they had to fight their corner.

The so-called Celtic Church, before St. Augustine of Canterbury made his takeover bid, had a better record. We know of a number of powerful abbesses who ran successful monastic institutions in Ireland, and the indications are that women had a higher status in the Celtic culture than in the Germanic one.

This patriarchal bias of organised Christianity is no longer acceptable in our time, and women are indeed finding their voice in the Church. A significant proportion of Anglican priests are women, and the first handful of women bishops have recently been appointed. The Roman Catholics have a long way to go, but their nuns are amongst the most vociferous in the demand for change. Having women in active role will change matters, and it will be difficult for some to adapt. (The Society of Friends — Quakers — have never suffered from this problem. Their women have been as active and powerful as the men since the sect came into being.)

Sex and sainthood

Anti-sexuality has been a blot upon the Church, and done immense damage. From St. Paul's grudging comment that 'it is better to marry than to burn' to St. Augustine of Hippo's rejection of his partner and their child; from St. Jerome's bizarre behaviour, through to the edict of Hildebrand (Pope Gregory VII) that renewed the largely defunct celibacy of the clergy; down to our own day, sex has been seen as problematic. With the controversy about contraception, and the long denial of widespread abuse of children by celibate priests, the message is that sex is trouble.

It seems ironic that one of the major Christian festivals — Christmas — celebrates the birth of the Christ child to a single mother, who was only rescued from disgrace by Joseph's intervention. At the same time, real life unmarried mothers have been treated with appalling rejection varying from social disapproval down to real cruelty.

Anti-sexuality is not unique to Christianity. It can be found lurking in corners of the other major world religions and elsewhere, even although it is not such a dominant theme.

99

Perhaps it represents a universal human aberration. What is it about?

Underlying it is the assumption of a split between the material world — seen as bad — and the spiritual world — seen as the ultimate good. It was a fashionable attitude in the Middle East at the time St. Paul was taking the Christian message to the Gentiles. It was central to the Manichean belief system — and St. Augustine of Hippo was for a time a Manichean as a young man, before his return to his mother's Christian faith.

It was also part of the Cathars' belief system. Catharism was a heretical Christian dualist movement that thrived in some areas of Southern Europe, particularly northern Italy and southern France between the 12th and 14th centuries. Cathar beliefs varied between communities because Catharism was initially taught by ascetic priests who had set few guidelines.

The idea of two Gods or principles, one being good and the other evil, was central to Cathar beliefs. The good God was the God of the New Testament and the creator of the spiritual realm, as opposed to the evil God, whom many Cathars and, particularly, their persecutors identified as Satan, creator of the physical world of the Old Testament.

All visible matter, including the human body, was created by this evil god; it was therefore tainted with sin. It seemed to offer a neat solution to the age-old problem of evil in the world. This was the antithesis of the Catholic Church's monotheism, whose fundamental principle was that there was only one God who created all things visible and invisible.

Cathars thought human spirits were the genderless spirits of angels trapped within the physical creation of the evil god, cursed to be reincarnated until the faithful achieved salvation through a ritual at the point of death called the *consolamentum*. However, the Church has always insisted that such an attitude is heretical.

It appeals, though, to a certain kind of personality — those we might label as schizoid. Schizoid personality disorder is characterised by a lack of interest in social relationships, a tendency towards a solitary lifestyle, secretiveness, emotional coldness, and apathy. Affected individuals may simultaneously demonstrate a rich, elaborate and exclusively internal fantasy world. This could also be looked on as an overactive imagination that was developed in early childhood.

Such people, probably as the result of severe stressing very early in life, retreat from the pain of living an embodied life and strive to live in the head. Their development is such that, if they have the intelligence, they tend to become intellectuals and find a positive niche as such, but their social and personal skills often remain underdeveloped. At the extreme end of the spectrum, celibacy is not a problem for them, because their emotional development has not reached the level that allows them to be sexually functional. Where they achieve some measure of relatedness, it tends to remain immature and unsatisfactory.

Such personalities have long found a safe haven within the Church which has allowed them a sense of identity and status. However, what does it say about the ministry they offer, when they are expected to comment on matters of which they have no direct experience, and from which they have turned away!

Also, at depth there is a deep anger and rejection of the mother who failed to protect them when at their most vulnerable — the mother who failed to ensure their safe welcome into the embodied world. This rejection colours all their relationships with the female sex, and can led to punitive, destructive behaviour.

The problem of parenthood

There is another group of people whose attitude towards sexuality tends to become distorted. These are personalities who are in many ways more developed than the schizoid. They are embodied, they have achieved a measure of mature sexuality, yet they opt for celibacy. What I believe they are rejecting is parenthood.

Until very recently sexual activity usually resulted in pregnancy and children. Rearing children takes a long time and much hard work. It involves the father having to commit to the livelihood which enables them to be fed and housed. He may find himself doing work which he would not have chosen.

For many, this is a worthwhile bargain. A good family life is what they prize, and they are content to play the necessary role and enjoy the satisfactions that come with it. Others have a different agenda. They are aware of their own innate potential which demands to be developed. They perceive, accurately, that rearing children necessitates that one puts one's own personal needs on one side in order to meet those of the immature and vulnerable. They know they cannot have it all; they have to choose.

In other cases they may be narcissistic, and while able to relate to others are not very sensitive to others' needs. These personalities do not actually have much to give. They are often charismatic, but as partners and parents they are emotionally depriving — they need it all for themselves.

However, both these groups are still sexually functional. Celibacy does not come easily. The woman remains the vessel of temptation. If they resort to prostitutes, the woman is a degraded and despised figure. The more intrusive their own sexuality, the harder they have to wrestle with it. It is difficult for them to accept where the tension comes from. Far easier to blame all women, and the drive of sexuality itself. One can see this scenario acted out time and again within the Church, and the lives of the saints offer many examples.

I have talked here of men. What of the women drawn into the anti-sexual culture of the Church? How did they reconcile themselves to it? Again, many were schizoid personalities, the retreat from an embodied life into a spiritual world a relief. They bore the often harsh demands of the material world with fortitude, expecting nothing better. However, it could make them harsh towards those in their care — the unmarried mothers, the orphans, the children to be educated. Too often they acted out, and inculcated the sense of guilt around sexuality into a younger generation.

I suspect those remarkable women who became impressive leaders in the Church, the abbesses of monastic institutions, came into the other category of people who deliberately chose to give up the possibility of parenthood in order to follow another creative path. How else could Hildegarde of Bingen become the creative human being she was.

Is celibacy easier for women? Perhaps women's sexuality is less insistent, more dependent on external stimulation for arousal. Perhaps it is more readily diverted into substitute maternal functions — caring, nursing, education. Perhaps. In many cases it worked, and the people developed and matured. In others one feels that the personalities shrivelled and soured. I doubt it was ever an easy path.

The struggle against sexual desire has so obsessed so many in the Church that Sin has become equated with sexual misdemeanours (as opposed to its original understanding as separation from God.) The question of why the Good Lord created us as sexual beings never seems to be asked. An error of judgment, an unfortunate necessity — from an omnipotent Deity? The mind boggles!

I see these attitudes as essentially blasphemous. In the past they may have had some positive social value in controlling the birth-rate in communities who could only afford to care for a limited number of children. It is easy for us to forget the ever-present threat of starvation in times past.

Now we have no excuse. Contraception has freed us from the inevitable link between sexual activity and pregnancy. In doing so we have created other problems — in the West we have tended to trivialise what is a fundamental and deeply meaningful human activity — and we need to address such issues. The Church still has to come to terms with this aspect of the human animal.

I am always uneasy at Christmas time. The festival of Christmas is surely the celebration of new life — whether one interprets that in Christian terms as the birth of the Christ child, the revelation of the Incarnation — or whether one sees it as the pagan winter festival, the turn of the year and the gradual return of the life-giving Sun. Either way, it celebrates the creative force at the heart of our universe and welcomes its manifestation in our lives.

At the same time, I feel we have little respect for the everyday miracle of creation. The Nativity is played out with the birth of each and every baby, and should be met with the same reverence and awe as the shepherds and the wise men brought to it.

In our current society, babies have become a commodity we choose or choose not to have — and then get very upset if we can't, as and when we want. We behave as if we have a right to them; and then all-too-often farm them out for others to care for while we pursue those all-important things of life we call work and career. We starve the midwifery service of money so there are too few of them to do their job as they would wish, we close down local hospitals ensuring that mothers-to-be have to travel long distances away from home to reach the maternity units. We deliver babies by Caesarian section far too often, to suit the convenience of everyone except the baby.

We encourage mothers to return to work as soon as they can. And since as mothers they have little respect or status or value in the wider community, they are all too often relieved to get back into an ambience where they feel they have significance.

The whole scenario is a disgrace. How dare we celebrate Christmas! We have lost our sense of what it is all about.

17. Sex

Sex is an affirmation of life. It is the means by which new life is brought into being. When we engage in sexual activity, it is the Life Force living us. To treat it as sinful or dirty, or as just part of our gross animal nature, is to my mind blasphemous and a denial of what Incarnation is all about.

If environmental conditions are threatening, the sexual drive can become more than usually insistent. We see heightened sexual activity between people at times of war, at times of bereavement, after external disasters. They can sometimes feel rather ashamed of their behaviour, not recognising it as a fundamental sign of hope for the future.

We see the same phenomenon in the plant kingdom. A plant will sometimes produce a bumper crop of flowers and fruit before dying. We make use of this tendency when we prune or root-prune a plant. It feels its existence threatened, so it fruits more copiously.

Human beings take a long time to mature, as do their capacities accordingly. The physical capacity for sexual expression becomes active in early teens, although it is possible to see precursors throughout the developmental years, from the loving feelings of the infant for its carers to the curiosity of the latency-age child.

Cultural distortions

When physical maturity is attained, the young person then has to cope with the expectations and limitations imposed upon its expression by the culture in which it lives. These are variable with time and place, but the sound young person is not so driven that they cannot observe and manage the tensions.

In our current Western society, within a framework of law, a certain license is allowed the adolescent young as they experiment with relationships. Other cultures are less permissive, and in a mixed society such as we have in the UK today, this can result in conflict and tensions.

Just as a tree can react to stress by producing an abnormally heavy crop of fruit, so we can note the human young exhibiting stress by its sexual behaviour. Girls will sometimes begin to menstruate unusually early for no obvious physical reason. Nine was the earliest in my personal experience.

It is the children of dysfunctional families who tend to become sexually active early in their young lives — hence the number of teenage pregnancies. They are too often looking for the love and attention they did not get as children, and which they crave in order to feel fully alive. They hope that sexual intimacy will provide it. Sadly, it all too often just perpetuates the deprivation into the next generation.

The course of sexual development can get distorted or perverted during the lengthy childhood years. Male sexuality seems more vulnerable to perversion, but this may be an illusion. The adult female sexual role requires a mood of acceptance, of acquiescence, which can be mistakenly perceived as passivity. When female sexuality becomes perverted, it tends to be less obvious than in the male. Louise Kaplan[1] writes in detail and persuasively about female sexual perversion, illuminating many aspects which tend not be labelled as such. Adult male sexuality demands a degree of pro-activity. Perversion of this drive is therefore more obvious to the observer.

Just as young ducklings can be persuaded to attach themselves to a human being as 'mother' so the immature young human can come to perceive inappropriate others as the focus of their sexual desires. A major body of Tinbergen's research[2] focused on what he termed *Supernormal Stimuli*. This was the concept that one could build an artificial object which was a stronger stimulus or releaser for an instinct than the object for which the instinct originally evolved.

- A certain class of Victorian men married within their own social group, but compulsively sought sexual pleasure with women of a lower class, who reminded them of their nursemaids and nannies.

- A father can be so sexually seductive to his small daughter that subsequently she will only be attracted to older men — father figures.

---

[1] Kaplan, Louise (1991) *Female Perversions: The Temptations of Madame Bovary*

[2] Nikolaas "Niko" Tinbergen FRS (1907 – 1988) was a Dutch ethologist and ornithologist who shared the 1973 Nobel Prize in Physiology or Medicine with Karl von Frisch and Konrad Lorenz for their discoveries concerning organisation and elicitation of individual and social behaviour patterns in animals.

- A boy is sexually abused by an older man. He subsequently abuses children of the age he himself was at that time.

This is admittedly an over-simplification of the often complex psychodynamics within the families concerned which leads to a pathological outcome. However, there is a point to be made about inappropriate fixation on the object of desire.

In considering sexual perversion, especially in its more shocking manifestations, it is important to recall the infantile and childish precursors of the slowly developing sexual capacity; and also to remember that sexuality at a fundamental level is about life — and death.

A basic precursor is the infant's experience of physical contact with its mother's body — the sensuous warmth and comfort which reassures the baby, newly thrust from the all-embracing containment of the womb, that it is safe and alive.

One only has to watch the vigorous infant when it is about to be put to the breast — it becomes excited at the prospect, and latches on to the nipple with evident satisfaction. If it has to wait for more than a brief period, it makes its distress known in no uncertain fashion. It behaves as if its survival is at stake, which literally it is.

Violence to partners

I feel that those cases of men who are violent towards their sexual partners represent a re-enactment of this infantile scenario by men who, at the time, have as little sense of their partner as a separate human being as has the baby of its mother. When we witness a frustrated baby having a strop, we can laugh sympathetically at its distress. When it is a large adult male with the same angry, destructive feelings, it is a different ball-game.

As in so much psychopathology, there is a repetition compulsion at work. Such men tend to choose partners who will behave in the same chronically frustrating, unsatisfying way that they experienced with their mothers. Insight is a long way from consciousness, and the outcome can be dire for both parties.

In a healthy family setting, the small child begins to experience protosexual feelings towards the carer of the opposite sex — what we have come to call the Oedipal phase of development. Small boys are sometimes heard to declare that they are going to marry their Mummy, small girls their Daddy. If this time in a child's life is handled with sympathetic tolerance, disillusion will finally set in as the child realises that the parent concerned already has a partner who will not be displaced. A phase of negativity towards the parent of the same sex often occurs, but in time this moderates as the child accepts reality and begins, instead, to identify with that parent.

If this phase has been handled wisely, the child will be left with some sense that it is loveable and that it will, in the future, find a sexual partner of its own. In due course, latency sets in which delays the onset of sexual maturation, and also provides a period during which social skills are learned and cognitive functions develop. Then puberty arrives, the biological clock triggers hormone production and the sexual drive becomes active.

What can go wrong? Because human maturation is such a lengthy process, the sexual trajectory is open to many pressures and influences. In order for sexual development to become 'normal' in the young adult, the innate biological needs must be met by a facilitating environment.

This can fail in various ways. There may be no one to function as the recipient of the small child's protosexual feelings because of absence or neglect.

The parent of the opposite sex may be rejecting of the child's tentative feelings — he or she may be mocked and made to feel foolish.

The same sex parent may be perceived as too threatening — too strict or disapproving — for the child to feel safe to express its longings. It can be made to feel that they are unacceptable, shameful or wicked.

Paedophilia

Where does such a child put its sexual feelings? Other children are safe, non-threatening and available. They may even enjoy the encounter. We are approaching the realm of paedophilia.

Professionals describing the personalities of paedophiles write of low self-esteem, impaired self-concept, poor social skills, impaired inter-personal functioning and elevated passive-aggressiveness. They also describe introversion, cognitive distortion and impaired inhibitory function. What emerges is a widespread picture of an inadequate, depriving environment during both childhood and latency.

We have become inured to the many complaints from the victims of former child abuse by Roman Catholic clergy. It has done immense damage to that Church, and destroyed its stronghold in Ireland. The Jimmy Savile affair has been shocking, and its ramifications are still echoing as other figures within the media are revealed as implicated in similar activities.

Jimmy Savile (1926-2011) was a hugely popular media personality and entertainer for many years. He appeared frequently on television, and raised a lot of money for charitable purposes. Because of his reputation he was given free access to hospitals and other institutions without serious question. It was only after his death that it became apparent that he was a serious and active paedophile who had grossly misused his position to escape detection. Some of his victims had indeed tried to complain but had been ignored by those in charge of protecting them.

We have known for some time that children's care homes have been used as a source of victims — as paedophilic brothels, a sickening thought. Now it seems that historically there was a paedophile ring involving senior members of our society, who at the time held public posts of considerable responsibility.

What is this all about?

We must distinguish those men who are attracted to prepubertal children from those drawn to very young women. 'Girls' in their teens can be enormously seductive towards father figures with little consciousness of what they are doing. We find it alien that in mediaeval Europe the age for marriage was legitimately and frequently 13-14. That was the recognition of a certain reality. In such cases today, we condemn the failure to maintain appropriate boundaries in those men who respond actively to what should preferably be dealt with as the Oedipal seduction and practising from very young women. However, these men strictly speaking are not paedophiles.

Behind a preference for very young girls is a fear of the adult woman. We under-estimate the universal fear of men for women, derived from their experience as babies of being totally dependent on a woman. This underlies the age-old battle for power between the sexes, down to the feminist movement of today.

In paedophilia proper it is the immaturity, the absence of sexuality, that is the attraction. What does it mean to these men? One can imagine — for the adult fixated on children as sexual objects — that their object choices may well arouse envy for what the victim has had, and what the offender has never experienced. I feel that they want to steal something from the child — to have for themselves what the child represents — a new beginning, uncontaminated innocence, the potential for wholeness that they have lost. They are also angry that the child has this 'something' they have lost, and want to punish it for its effrontery in possessing it. One can only imagine the maelstrom of feelings that may get stirred — desire, shame, hurt, rage, the wish to engulf and incorporate the loved one, massive denial of that part of oneself — the feelings too painful to manage.

I have wondered if, when a child is killed by a paedophile, the offender is at some level acting-out what was done to him. He is the child in whom life was killed — the living core of himself murdered. It is indeed a matter of life and death.

At the deepest level, in paedophilic encounters, I suspect there may be collusion between the deprived child-in-the-adult, and the real-life child looking for parental warmth and affection. It would be deeply sad were not the end results so damaging.

Is this psychopathology more widespread today than hitherto, or are we just becoming more aware of it? We cannot know. Certainly, during a period of social perversion[3] such as we have lived through in the last fifty years, with its accompanying denial of difference, erosion of boundaries and disregard of traditional values, it is hardly surprising if there has been more acting-out of sexual deviancy.

There is, and has been, a lot of hidden deprivation amongst very small children whose basic needs for warmth and affection have been denied them by their carers. The Truby King regime for infants of the early 20th century was cold and unfeeling. The current fashion of mothers returning to work soon after childbirth is, I fear, storing up trouble for the future. There is a reluctance to accept the reality that our young are very immature at birth, very vulnerable, and take a long time to mature. No cultural fashion, no clever technology, no artificial feeding programmes, can obliterate our basic mammalian inheritance. Our young need consistent and continuous emotional warmth as well as physical care. It is time we faced that fact.

---

[3] I am using the term 'perversion' in its psychoanalytical meaning derived from the work of Janine Chasseguet-Smirgel.

18. Venus *et al*

I am looking at a photograph of the so-called Venus of Willendorf. She is just one of many similar prehistoric figures which have been unearthed by palaeontologists. The suggestion is that our ancestors of that time worshipped a Mother goddess, whom these statuettes represent.

To call her Venus has always felt to me to be a misnomer, implying as it does beauty and sexual attraction. I cannot believe that our ancestors had such a different aesthetic sense from ourselves, since that aesthetic sense is so clearly derived from basic biology and the human form. Whatever meaning one gives to these figurines, seductive they are not.

When I suddenly notice my own 80-year old body naked in the mirror, I am struck by the resemblance. This little statue surely represents an old woman who has borne and suckled many children. Was it perhaps created in gratitude to one whose fecundity was literally vital to the survival of her tribe? After all, the planetary dominance of our species began with her and her ilk.

However, in our time, women's fecundity is no longer so prized. We have been such a successful animal that we are in danger of overwhelming the capacity of our planet to support us. Now, we seriously need to limit our breeding.

At the same time, we have fallen in love with our power to control so many aspects of our lives, and we imagine that procreation is one of them. Convinced we can decide when and how we have our children, we use contraception to avoid or delay pregnancy. The first pregnancy may be left so late that there are difficulties in achieving fertility. All sorts of invasive techniques are then used to give back what was spurned, and recently we have seen the curious phenomenon of women opting to give birth at an age beyond their natural menopause, while their contemporaries are already into grandmotherhood.

Marginal babies

All this in a patriarchal society which values women as well as men not for what they *are* but for what they *do*, what they achieve in the outside world — their work, their careers. Women's capacity to give birth is denigrated so that we become apologetic about our role. To be 'just a housewife and mother' is to be negligible.

Having a baby is something to be squeezed into one's life with minimal fuss. One is expected to go on working throughout pregnancy, and to return to it after the least possible time off. There is no general recognition of the profundity of the experience — both physiologically and psychologically — for the woman, and for her partner too if he is at all involved.

Midwifery services are stretched to breaking point, mothers and babies are returned home after the briefest possible hospital confinement to circumstances where frequently there is quite inadequate support. Health visitors are thin on the ground. In these days when extended families are often widely scattered, there is a void, when what is needed is a supportive network to free the mother for her new role.

The vital importance of the early days and weeks for the vulnerable human neonate and its parents is somehow denied. Yes, our post-natal statistics are good, physically our babies survive and grow, but there is no recognition that the future mental health of the individual is founded on those earliest experiences. Too often the needed continuity and consistency of care is replaced by anxious and chaotic multiple care-taking.

Fecundity threatens us

Globally, we have a problem. The fecundity of our species has resulted in over-population of our planet, and ultimately our survival as a species is in question unless we can respond appropriately. I suspect that the denigration in our society of women's primary function is an unconscious social attempt to put a brake on our rate of reproduction.

We saw a similar mechanism at work in the Middle Ages when a significant proportion of the population were in Holy Orders and celibate. At that time, too many mouths to feed quickly brought starvation. There are signs that before long we too may be facing a global shortage of adequate foodstuffs, with all the threats to political stability that that would bring in its wake. David Attenborough made the point in a recent interview[1]:

> 'We are a plague on the Earth. It's coming home to roost over the next 50 years or so. It's not just climate change. It's sheer space, places to grow food for this enormous

---

[1] Interview for the *Radio Times* (Jan. 26 — Feb.1, 2013)

horde. Either we limit our population growth or the natural world will do it for us, and the natural world is doing it for us right now.

We keep putting on programmes about famine in Ethiopia; that's what's happening. Too many people there. They can't support themselves — and it is not an inhuman thing to say, it's the case. Until humanity manages to sort itself out and get a coordinated view about the planet, it's going to get worse and worse.'

However, the current and largely unconscious forces at work to limit our reproductive rate are achieving the worst possible outcome, satisfactory to no one. Undoubtedly, the best way to limit population growth has been found to be the education of women. It gives them other interests in life, other sources of satisfaction and status, and frees their energies to be creative in other directions.

Children — treasuring the few

However, it seems to me to be vital that the fewer children we have, the more important it is that they are treated in such a way as to develop their full potential as human beings. There are certain inescapable facts. We are very immature and therefore vulnerable at the time of birth. We take a very long time to reach maturity compared with most mammals. Both these facts make heavy demands upon the carers.

As babies, we need a consistency and continuity of care which comes most readily to the ordinary devoted mother. She needs to be free to give that care, and to be given the support she needs in order to offer it to her infant for as long as she feels the need is there. This makes demands upon those around her. She cannot do it adequately on her own. She needs to be able to allow herself to retreat into that 'primary maternal preoccupation' which enables her to be sensitive, and to respond appropriately, to her baby's non-verbal needs.

She needs a partner who will not only support her, but who will gradually play his part in bringing the external world to the child as it develops the capacity to be interested in it and interact with it, and who can help to gently dissolve the intense mother/child bond when the time is right. The child needs parents who are willing to stay together, and work together, for the long period of time needed before the child becomes an independent adult.

It is a tall order, demanding a measure of emotional stability and maturity. It demands a set of values which puts the welfare of the younger generation before one's own narcissistic needs, and in the face of many current social demands. This is something many ordinary parents do out of love — for the child, for each other, out of their own innate sense of what is needed, and what is most important in life. We need a society which will recognise the value, the vital importance of what they do.

At present they too often have to struggle against social attitudes and expectations which leaves them fighting battles on several fronts. It is hardly surprising if they retreat from the tensions into the 'safer' world of work, of career development, muddling through the years of child-rearing as best they can. Is it surprising that the divorce rate is as high as it is?

What we need is a perspective which allows us to move towards a goal of reducing our population pressure without denigrating the fundamental, and deeply satisfying, human function of procreation. The current social attitudes are giving us the worst of 'solutions.'

We are in danger of rearing too many people who are inadequately nurtured, damaged in the process, and unable to fully contribute to the general good. Yes, some people make admirable lives out of a poor beginning, but there is also a lot of unacknowledged, unproductive and unnecessary misery. Too many of our young women are confused about their role in life, and what are their emotional needs as women. There is a danger of them subsiding into chronic discontent.

Psychologist Steve Biddulph[2] writes 'There's now a cluster of really serious problems that are hugely on the up for girls. One in five will experience a serious psychological disorder before reaching adulthood. They are a lot more anxious, they are more likely to self-harm, they are more prone to bullying, they are binge-drinking and they are more likely to be at risk of promiscuous sexual behaviour. Girls are more stressed and depressed than they have ever been before.'

Meanwhile too many men have little concept of fathering, or indeed of what is the role of an adult male. While there may be relief — a sense of freedom — in evading the burdens of family life, the end result is all too often a failure of emotional development — of being stuck in an adolescent immaturity which contaminates the rest of their functioning.

Somewhere along the line we have lost the plot. We need a new perspective. We need a change of values.

---

[2] Biddulph S. (2013) *Raising Girls* Harper Collins

19. Roots of sexism

Our eldest granddaughter tells me that sexism is still active in her workplace. So far it has not held her back. With a PhD. under her belt and some years in academic research, she is well qualified against discrimination, and with her energy and enthusiasm she is flourishing in her present university administration role. However, her remarks led me to thinking about this still widespread phenomenon which the years of active feminism have only dented.

Male ambivalence

All men have some ambivalence towards women. It derives from their infancy when they were totally dependent on a woman for their survival. She had the power to make life heaven or hell. Insofar as that experience was good, the boy then has to break that initial powerful attachment to mother in order to become a man and seek his own woman. It takes a mother with some maturity to give her small son the loving care he needs, and to then let him go as is appropriate. A sound husband and father can help both parties in the process.

This is the best possible scenario, leaving only a small residue of wariness of the powerful woman. Where that experience was less happy, there is greater ambivalence towards women, with outright hostility at worst.

Older sisters — and their friends — can be a formative influence, for good or ill. Male pride in the young boy is a sensitive plant which can easily be dented. One way of protecting it is to ignore the other sex, or to treat them as inferior and useless.

One might have thought that co-education would help to counter-act this tendency. Perhaps it has. However, since girls tend to be relatively more mature than boys of the same age, their greater success in the classroom has been challenging. Our education system favours those literary abilities in which girls tend to excel. Also, the predominance of women teachers and the relative scarcity of men in the profession is not helpful to boys.

The male workplace has many characteristics of the hunting, warring band. An innate part of such a group is the competitive struggle for one's place in the hierarchy. Again, male narcissism is a powerful driver, and the less sound the individual, the more powerfully this operates. For such men, women have no place in the group. It is essentially a 'boy's game' and they want to preserve it as such.

For all men, women bring the challenge of their sexuality — to be appreciated, welcomed or rejected. Some men find it a tiresome distraction — they don't want to have to deal with their own reactions to it in the work setting. They resent it and those who personify it. Their subsequent behaviour can be appalling, as women Members of Parliament have testified.

Lastly, I think many men can only function well 'out there' with the background support of a woman — a domestic Personal Assistant. They would be loath to admit it, but the need can be great. They are threatened not only by the competence of the working women, but by the implied threat that she may not be around, or even want to cater for their needs. It is frightening at a deep level. When people are frightened they hit out in all sorts of ways, direct and subtle. For some men, women need to be 'kept in their place.' It is actually pathetic, largely unacknowledged but very real.

If men are challenged by the changing patterns of our cultural life, so are women. Women's only hope of achieving their potential, their ambitions and aspirations is to produce sons who can grow into mature, sound men and cooperative partners. This requires a period of devoted care from the mothers of sons (and from fathers who provide an active role model.) Without that good foundation, these tensions can never be resolved to a level that allows room for the creativity of both sexes.

Can we have it all?

Legislation can only do so much. Time allows custom and practice to develop, and we have already come a long way. War-time experience changed much for both sexes. Out of necessity, women took over traditional male work and functions, and many discovered abilities, self-respect and a freedom previously unknown. However, the traditional patterns of good parenting were inevitably interrupted, domestic skills were denigrated, extended families dispersed as social and geographical mobility increased.

Since then the nuclear family has become devalued by fashion, and put under stress. The immature young have too often been short-changed in the process. As a society, we are reluctant to face that reality and its implications.

Ultimately we have to respect the biological given and work with it. It won't go away — whatever the contemporary fashion would have us believe!

20. Permission to go, permission to grow

Among my collection of cuttings is a picture, a reproduction of a painting. It came as the front page of a National Trust magazine, and if it were in better condition I would have framed it and hung it on my wall. Alas, it is too tattered — but it called to me powerfully when I first met it, and it calls to me still.

The female artist

The original of my print was painted by Dora Carrington, who was one of a group of very talented young artists training at the Slade School of Art just prior to World War One. She was arguably the lively epicentre of a group which included Richard Nevinson, Paul Nash, Mark Gertler and Stanley Spencer. Several of them fell in love with her, and argued over her. She had a tempestuous relationship with Mark Gertler, but eventually formed a deep and lasting attachment to Lytton Strachey of Bloomsbury fame.

Although, by all accounts, she was compulsively creative, she has left only a small legacy of easel paintings, and those almost entirely in private hands. It has been suggested that her tragedy was that neither Ralph Partridge who she married, nor Lytton Strachey, encouraged her to paint. Instead she devoted her considerable energies to making a home for, and nurturing, the hypochondriac Strachey. Six months after his early death, she killed herself.

I was intrigued by this word 'encouraged'. Carrington said of herself that she liked men, but hated being a woman. Perhaps the fact that Strachey was a flagrant homosexual was part of his attraction for her — she did not have to play the sexual counterpart to him. Yet it seems to me that it was just her 'womanliness' that led her to betray her artistic talent. No one stopped her painting; she was not a woman anyone could have stopped from doing her own thing! Instead, she chose to use her energies in a traditional womanly way as homemaker and nurse.

The early feminists have depicted women's historical under-achievement in the arts as the result of male oppression. A recent series of television programmes, fronted by Professor Amanda Vickery, presented this viewpoint very powerfully[1].

There is a case to be made — the attitude of composer Gustav Mahler towards his wife Alma was probably not unique in their time. Alma Mahler[2] was by contemporary accounts a talented musician and composer. After their marriage Gustav infamously forbade her to continue her interest in 'his' sphere, but to confine herself to the domestic role — and she accepted his diktat! She never returned to her musical activi-

---

[1] *The Story of Women and Art* BBC2. May 16th, 23rd, 30th, 2014. Amanda Vickery is Professor of Early Modern History at Queen Mary's College, London.

[2] Alma Mahler (1879 - 1964) was a highly intelligent and beautiful woman. After Mahler's death she married Walter Gropius (1915), founder of the Bauhaus Movement, and subsequently the novelist Franz Werfel (1929). She was also involved with many other major figures of her cultural world. The artists Gustav Klimt and Oskar Kokoschka were among those with whom she had affairs.

ties even after his death, leaving one to wonder how important it actually was to her by that time.

Certainly, of the handful of significant women artists from earlier times, it is notable that many of them had fathers who were artists, and who encouraged their daughters as if they were sons. However, I wonder if it is not just as much women's own innate tendencies that undermine their potential artistic achievements.

Colluding in exploitation

Women's traditional skills as wife, mother and homemaker have been so basic to life, so necessary for survival, let alone civilised living, that they have been taken for granted and barely acknowledged. One could say, with some justification, that they have been exploited. However, I am suggesting that it has been all too easy, often necessary, for the women to collude in that exploitation.

It is only recently, as we live longer, are wealthier and have fewer children, that the possibility of exercising other skills has become a reality for most. Do women need encouragement to let go some of that traditional role — or do we perhaps need permission to do so without struggling with guilt? In the past, I suspect some women opted for the religious life for just this reason.

Change is threatening even when welcome. We like to think that we live in a world that is stable, but the reality is that it is always changing. We too are continually changing. We grow up, we mature, we age. The very cells in our body are continually dying and being replaced. We adapt for the most part without being overly conscious of the flux of life.

Yet, because we are social animals, because we are caught up in a nexus of relationships, we are continually adapting to the change in others as well as ourselves. We watch our young grow up, we watch our parents age and die, we experience our contemporaries dying. We have to accept these realities. It is not always easy or comfortable, and we can make it more or less difficult and uncomfortable by our own attitudes and behaviour. We need to accept — to give tacit permission to ourselves and others — for these changes to take place, not to battle the inevitable. Easier said than done!

Timely death and birth

When people are dying, it is a recognised phenomenon that they will often hang on until a certain event has occurred — a wedding, an anniversary, a birth in the family. Once this has occurred, they can give themselves permission to go — often when their nearest and dearest have crept away, and they are finally alone. At the other end of life, the initiation of the birth process seems to occur by some tacit physiological agreement between mother and infant. Hormonal levels drop; both are ready for the change.

A woman was in labour for four days before a forceps delivery rescued the baby — in the nick of time, as by then it was blue! There was no very obvious reason for the prolonged labour and the baby was quite small. Subsequently this mother had great difficulty in letting her child grow up and become separate from her. She was also a great hoarder — to a pathological degree in old age. Clearly this inability to let go was a deep-seated character trait. — probably the result of early deprivation in a large family, where she had little she could claim as her own.

128

Mothers of small children who are comfortable with their role, can wish to prolong the phase of babyhood. The total love and dependency of the very young gives one a unique sense of value and significance. However, the time comes when the small child has to turn away from mother towards the outside world, as its maturational potential drives it. It needs mother's permission to do so, and father's encouragement can be vital to both. The mother needs the man's permission to let go her total immersion in the role. Another baby can be the answer! Refusal to do so inhibits the child's development.

Adolescents are often experienced as tiresome and difficult. I suspect that this occurs so that, when they do finally leave home, there is relief on both sides! Truth to tell, this separation is fraught with ambivalence for both generations. The young need to establish their own lives but are fearful of leaving the safety and support of home; the parents are anxious for them, and for themselves without them. The young need permission, and encouragement, to take the plunge.

They also need to feel that their parents can survive their going — more difficult if home is fraught. I have noticed that it is the parents who, for whatever reason, have missed much of their children's growing up years, who are often the ones most reluctant to let them go. They feel they have been deprived of something, as they have, and find it difficult to accept that it is now too late to retrieve it.

A time of possibilities

This is the time — when the young have flown the nest — that possibilities really open up for women, especially given our now lengthy expectation of life. It is a time of considerable re-adjustment for both the women and the menfolk. They need to work together. The men perhaps need permission, and en-couragement, to work less arduously than when they had a growing family to support, and to develop those talents that had to be put on one side. Some find they enjoy taking over some of the woman's activities — many men enjoy cooking, others gardening. Whatever, it is a time of change for both, and needs to be negotiated together if the relationship is to flourish.

If one is gifted with a particular, compelling talent, the frustra-tions of the child-rearing years can be difficult. Both parents need permission from the other to keep that talent nurtured, at least minimally, so that it can more readily be taken up when the time is right. Again, encouragement is vital. It is too easy, under the pressures of daily life, for both parties to col-lude in ignoring what is not immediately needed.

So, I think it is not men the oppressors, men the enemy, who are to blame for the paucity of women artists in the past, but those factors of basic biology and survival with which we all struggle. Without the traditional work of women, the human race would not have flourished, and the men could not have achieved what they did achieve. However unwelcome the idea, society needed women to stay in their traditional role.

Now that work is needed less, or for a shorter part of one's life-span, where does that leave us? Challenged, for sure!

In the past, women had to choose: religious or secular, mar-ried or single, childless or family. Now we want it all! What-ever our decisions, there is a price to be paid. Perhaps we need to encourage our girls, our young women, to think a little more about the matter.

Perhaps, too, there is a sense in which we all need permission, social permission, the permission of our community, to become what we have it in us to be. We need permission to fulfil our basic biological needs, to be immature as children, to be risk-taking young adults, to be pre-occupied mothers, functional and authoritative fathers; then in due course to be old and tired — and to be allowed to look it — and to go when the time has come.

We also need space from the world's daily business to develop that potential which creates new things, new ideas, new ways at looking at the world, the art which refreshes the soul. It is not a matter of more time, more money, more anything (except perhaps imagination.) It is matter of allowing and using what we have — to become what we have it in us to be.

It is — it can only succeed as — a joint endeavour.

21. Women in religion

An elegant, still glamorous woman of retirement age was speaking. She was talking of how, in all the major religions across the globe, women were finding their voice.

Within the Christian tradition we now have women priests, and Anglican women bishops are likely to be a very ordinary thing in the near future[1]. The Quakers have never had a gender problem, and their women have been as active and vociferous as the menfolk since the sect came into being in the 17th century. If the Roman church is lagging behind, their nuns are amongst the liveliest voices demanding change.

The world outside Christendom

However, there is now apparently a widespread and powerful movement in Buddhism of women organising themselves to become educated and active in the religious domain. In Northern China, where there is a Muslim community, a group of women have created a women-only mosque. All of this was cause to rejoice to someone who was of that generation of feminists who had fought hard, and with considerable success, for women's rights.

I linked it with another lecture I had heard recently which suggested, with impressive and irrefutable statistics, that the

---

[1] By Easter 2015 the Anglican communion in the UK had four women bishops.

birthrate across the globe, even in densely populated Asia and Bangladesh, is now on average two per parental couple. It appears we are out of date in our anxieties about the global birth-rate.

It seems to me that both phenomena are the product of reliable, cheap, readily available contraception, and the liberation that this has brought to women — the freeing of time and energy from the demands of repeated pregnancies and child-rearing. With it comes the possibility of developing lives and interests in ways that could only have been day-dreams hitherto.

The prison gates

A member of our group told us of how disapproving and inhibiting her mother had been to her own attempts to lead a full life, and how destructive that had been to her as a young woman. It had come as a surprise to her to learn recently that her mother, now in her eighties, had played a significant and active role during the 1939-45 war, and had worked for a time within MI5. It was as if, with marriage and motherhood, the prison gates had clanged shut and that lively woman had got lost. I have met other women who have felt similarly, and resented their subsequent lives.

Yet in truth it is not the role that is the problem, but the perception of that role. If being 'just a wife and mother' has no status, if it is seen as something any fool can do, a cop-out from the real world of work, then it is hardly surprising if some women feel cheated and embittered. I argue that bearing and rearing children is probably the most important job in the world. It is about creating people — the next generation.

Running a home is providing the stage upon which family life is acted out. It requires not only time and hard work, but a capacity for containment of the emotional tensions that develop in any group of people, a flexibility to adjust to ever changing circumstances, to make judgments, to multi-task, to offer love in often difficult situations, to be creative in a continual low-key fashion, often making something out of very little. It is very demanding. Like many jobs, it teaches one all kinds of skills, and reveals aspects of oneself one didn't know one had.

Sexuality and child-bearing can be an intensely spiritual experience. It can add a whole dimension to one's religious thinking. It is certainly an opportunity to practise that love and compassion which is at the heart of all religion. It should be recognised as such, not despised.

What has changed is the time scale involved. As two children per parental couple becomes the norm, the proportion of a woman's adult life given over to the mothering role is decreased. Of course, one goes on feeling responsibility and (hopefully) affection for one's children, one goes on offering support when needed. However, in most cases the bulk of the task is done while the woman still has health and energy for other things.

A new work pattern

I would like to see a culture develop in which women can have a different work pattern from men — a pattern which allows them the crucial years at home with their young if they choose to have them, but which enables them to return gradually to previous work, or provides the opportunity to set out on a new career.

It is in no one's interests to insist that women follow the male working pattern in the professions, as at present. Too often the young women who attempt it are ridiculously stressed, or their children are short-changed, or they give up their legitimate aspirations and feel they have failed or betrayed themselves and their education. An alternative attempt at a solution is to leave child-bearing so late that they tend to run into problems of fertility.

In fact, by the time they have reached their middle years they have acquired, hopefully, some emotional maturity, all kinds of management skills, and will still have 25 years of working life ahead even given the current age of retirement.

I speak of professional women because it is in this group that one sees the tensions at their most acute, and the sense of waste is greatest. I can also recall a patient whose mother worked before marriage in a shop selling gramophone records. She remembered it as the happiest time of her life, and bitterly regretted its loss. Her resentment was a heavy burden for her son to bear, and interfered with his subsequent ability to commit to a relationship.

The issue is being addressed to some small degree in the re-entry of medical personnel after a career break. We need a whole lot more fresh thinking on the matter. I watch the younger women being both more realistic and more vociferous in their demands for a full life and a fuller use of their skills. The better educated they are, the more they expect something realistically attuned to their potential, to their life as it is actually lived.

However, they can only achieve this with the understanding and support of their menfolk. The first generation of feminists were intent on fighting their corner, and tended to see men as the enemy. I don't believe that this can ultimately work. Apart from other issues, men are generally larger, stronger and more single-minded than women, and in a straight fight are likely to win.

Women are vulnerable during their child-rearing years and need their menfolk as providers and reliable support; the children need their fathers as role models; sound, mature men want to perform these roles, and gain satisfaction from doing so. This is how good functional families work.

This means educating our boys better as to their role. It means rearing small boys to be sound human beings. A man who carries a deprived and angry small child within him cannot do the job that is needed. A man whose mother resented the appropriate demands he made upon her when himself young and vulnerable will not be sympathetic to what his wife is asking. Dysfunctional families breed dysfunctional families.

'Just an ordinary wife and mother' . who is fooling whom! Women finding their voice — yes. As women. As spiritual beings. As the talented whole of who they are. As the Good Lord created them.

Apologia

The following chapters were written with a Quaker audience in mind — and it shows! However, I have included them since I feel they communicate something of the flavour of contemporary Quaker thinking — a much-needed perspective in a world where religious conflict and fundamentalism is all too prevalent.

22. The meek shall inherit the earth

This was not a notion that appealed to me when young. Instead I rather envied those who were self-confident enough to demand others' attention, to assert their needs, to be at the centre of social gatherings.

I was recently looking at a book about the business world — not, I must add, my usual reading matter! In it the author, Harvard professor, Clayton M. Christensen, describes what he sees as a repetitive cycle in which companies create a good reputation, grow steadily to great success, then in a very brief time collapse into nothingness[1].

These successful companies flourished because they gave their customers what they wanted, and they concentrated on producing products which were ever better, more sophisticated, more elegant — and inevitably — more expensive. Their customers loved them, their shareholders loved the sales figures, the stock market loved them. They were the accountant's dream.

When some small, amateurish enterprises began to make simpler, more limited, cruder artefacts which did some of the work of the sophisticated products, they were ignored as beyond consideration. Apart from anything else, there was far too little profit to be made from these new toys. However,

---

[1] Christensen, C.M. (1997) *The Innovator's Dilemma.* Harvard Business School Press

what these hitherto successful companies failed to take on board was that the simpler products were being bought by customers because they were cheap, and yet good-enough for the purposes many had in mind. For some, their very simplicity was an asset.

By the time the big boys woke up to the fact that their business was being undermined, it was too late. They had lost the market. By failing to take notice and support some new ideas heralding change, they had lost the plot.

A striking example is IBM, which dominated world manufacture of computer hardware for many years. The name still flourishes, but it has become a quite different kind of business. Modern versions of the once world-renowned IBM products — PCs and Intel-based servers — are made in China by Lenovo, now one of the world's top three computer makers. The list no longer includes IBM, whose story is only one of many similar examples.

The fall of empires

One could extrapolate into the political domain. That power which terrorised the world for much of my lifetime — the Soviet Union — no longer exists. Its collapse was surprising and swift. In his recent book, the historian Norman Davies[2] writes of the many former empires which have subsequently disappeared and are largely forgotten. Who now thinks of Sweden, of Lithuania, as the great military powers they once were.

The Soviet Union collapsed because it failed to care properly for its infra-structure, while spending a major proportion of

---

[2] Davies, N. (2011) *Vanished Kingdoms* Allen Lane

its wealth on the means to make war. Although a few perceptive individuals may have seen through the blustering facade, for most onlookers the collapse of the USSR was unexpectedly and dramatically sudden.

One could even develop a similar argument for the collapse of the Western Roman Empire. Their farming methods were so exploitive of the land that the food supplies to the city of Rome had to be brought in from further and further afield. Eventually even the bread basket that was North Africa became exhausted.

What has Christensen to say?

A number of reflections follow from Christensen's book. One is to note that we live in a world that is always changing. Nothing stands still. Nothing, however stable it seems, lasts forever and we have to be ready to adapt to change.

Another is that it is vital to look after infra-structure. In a society, that means ensuring food supplies, adequate housing, sanitation, power supplies etc. — all areas in which the Soviet Union failed dismally. Another is caring and nurturing the young, since they are the future. In a business, this means nurturing new ideas, listening to the younger generation, putting resources into the research and development that are necessary for long-term health.

While our larger geographical neighbours are flailing wildly under the tensions within the Eurozone, it is interesting that those societies which rate most highly on the scale of happiness are the small ones — Norway, Denmark, Holland. They have always been too poor to develop grandiose aspirations, but have managed to use their limited natural resources to provide a comfortable and equitable life-style for their populations.

Christensen, now a grandparent, is entertaining in his comments on how seductive it is to find excuses to work long hours, to stay in the office to get some project finished, to give oneself a sense of having achieved something positive, instead of going home to the unstructured anarchy of family life. He points out that actually time spent with one's growing children, sharing their current concerns, is building those relationships which determine their future and yours. Ultimately that is far more important than a few hours more in the workplace. Reading between the lines, one is driven to wonder if he had to be taught that truth by his wife's determination — and against some resistance!

In the tale of large and small businesses, I am reminded of the dinosaurs and their fate. There is more than one theory as to why these creatures became extinct, but one possibility I find intriguing. While they were rampaging around the earth, some tiny mammals — our remote ancestors — were foraging unnoticed in the undergrowth. They found dinosaur eggs to be an excellent source of food, and because of that the reptiles' ability to reproduce was crucially undermined.

Within the Society of Friends (Quakers) we sometimes lament and feel anxious about our relatively small numbers compared with those of many other Christian denominations, let alone other faiths. I prefer to think of us as like those small animals in the dinosaur age, going about our busy lives, doing what needs to be done, often unaware of what we may be inadvertently bringing about, or what foundations we might be laying down for our descendants. Not prone to grandiose schemes, respecting the fundamentals of daily life, we have managed to adapt to social change, while continuing to value as primary our group experience of the numinous.

Now at the other end of my life, I am able to believe that maybe, indeed, the meek shall inherit the earth.

23. Quaker theology

From time to time throughout history there arises the occasional remarkable human being who has the capacity to see the world as it actually is. I would include in this group all the founders of the great world religions — Gautama, Moses, Jesus of Nazareth, Mohammed.

Their experience seems to them to be so exciting, so awe-inspiring, so mind-blowing that they want to communicate it to those around them. They try to put words to it using the language, the metaphors, the images and concrete examples of their own time and culture — and this is the beginning of a new religion.

Insofar as their listeners have shared something of the same experience, the words communicate and are understood. For those who are less developed in this dimension, all too soon the words themselves become sacred, fixed, and are clung to as embodying the infinite wisdom. Ritual and dogma are developed, and soon all becomes set in stone.

Before long we get small boys chanting the Scriptures by rote as in Islam, or co-religionists torturing and killing each other because they use the wrong words or ritual, as in Christianity. Somewhere along the way they have lost the plot!

Not in the manner of Friends

I think Quakerism is unique in that, at its centre, is the concept of continuing revelation. While respecting them, we do not feel ourselves to be bound by what our forebears decided. We expect to re-formulate our central ideas, hence the practice of occasionally revising our handbook, *Faith and Practice.* From time to time we modify the way we manage our gatherings.

It gives us freedom. It can also evoke anxiety. I have known enquirers made extremely anxious by both the silence in Meeting and the absence of ritual. I myself have great affection for my old copy of *Faith and Practice* — 1960 vintage — and have never quite warmed to the later 1995 one, a comment on my own conservatism!

Also, our flexibility does bring with it the danger that we can be unduly influenced by the passing fashions of our time. During a certain era, when Nonconformity was at its peak, Quakers began to look like just another Nonconformist sect. We had travelling ministers who preached sermons, and publicly uttered moral judgments.

Today, we reflect some of the attitudes of our recent perverse society with its erosion of boundaries, denial of difference, and reluctance to exercise leadership and appropriate authority. [1] This latter characteristic has made it difficult to find members willing to take on the structural roles of the Society — a problem currently widespread amongst professional or-

---

[1] I am using the term 'perverse' in a technical (psychoanalytical) sense. I do not wish to imply moral disapproval or judgment. I have written about it in my book *Fatal Flaws (2012)*.

ganisations. Fortunately, that same flexibility allows us to recover our mistakes in due course.

Becoming a Friend

What brings us into the Society of Friends? We each have a different path. During my painful and difficult adolescence I had, with some frequency, an experience which was totally at odds with my usual depressed state of mind. It was a sudden revelation of the unity of all things, of feeling at one with that universe, of overwhelming joy and safety, and of being upheld. It kept me sane, and helped me survive. It was the experience I later recognised in the words of Julian of Norwich, 'But all shall be well, and all shall be well, and all manner of thing shall be well.'

I never talked about it to anyone then. It was only subsequently, when chance, in the guise of a friendly Quaker, brought me into a Meeting for Worship, that I realised there were other people who had experienced that kind of illumination. I discovered Evelyn Underhill, and the mystical writings of other times and other cultures. Much later, in reading about the research of the Alister Hardy Society, I learned that it is actually a very common, if not universal experience in varying degrees of intensity.

Some people prefer to give it a non-religious explanation, or a naturalistic one. In my understanding, everything — including the miraculous — has a naturalistic explanation, even if we cannot always locate it. The words seem to me irrelevant — it is an experience of the numinous, outside time, when we touch the fringe of eternity. It is, I believe, an innate characteristic of being human.

In a recent article in *Friends' Quarterly (2014 — 2)* Hugh Rock argued that our corporate action is what defines us as a group. I would argue that the action is secondary to the insight; it is the fruit of the Spirit. I am reminded of the Anglican saying[2]: 'Good works not undertaken in Faith partake of the nature of Sin.' Once one has a glimpse of what it is all about, then the way clarifies and one's actions follow. We may each have to make an individual response dependent on our innate temperament, talents, and particular circumstances, and that is not always easy as one negotiates conflicting demands and loyalties — but the perception, the need, the shared discrimination comes first.

Continuing revelation

Our tradition of continual revelation gives us great freedom and power in today's confusing world, where there is both an enormous spiritual hunger and a widespread dissatisfaction with formalised religious practice. How should we use it?

We could use the media to greater advantage. I have been pleased to see the occasional advert in the press recently, but we could do so much more using professional PR skills. If we did, we might evoke an avalanche of response, and would need to brace ourselves to meet it. Is this what we want as a group? Enthusiasm has been suspect since the days of James Naylor — with good reason!

James Naylor (1516-60) was one of the first generation of Quakers. A charismatic and eloquent figure, he was the most prominent of the so-called 'Valiant Sixty' who travelled the

---

2 (1662) 'Thirty nine articles' *Book of Common Prayer*

realm, preaching the tenets of this newly-formed Christian sect and attracting a devoted following. However, he also attracted the unwelcome attentions of the civil authorities when, in Bristol in 1556, he re-enacted Jesus' entry into Jerusalem riding on a donkey.

He was imprisoned and harshly punished for blasphemy, and there was a breach with George Fox, the founder of the Society of Friends, who felt his messianic enthusiasm had become a dangerous embarrassment. Beware the lure of the charismatic would-be leader in religion as in politics.

Whatever — the creative ferment is active within our Society. How can we use it? What form is it going to take?

24. Quakerism — where next?

In her 2013 James Backhouse lecture — *A Quaker Astronomer Reflects* — Jocelyn Bell Burnell commented that in other age she would probably have been regarded as a mystic.

The same could be said of many who find their spiritual home within the Society of Friends. Indeed, within the community of the Christian Church, I see Quakers as the group who nowadays most embody the mystical tradition. That is not to say that one cannot find mystics in other denominations — I have personally known a few — but the significance of the Quaker Meeting for Worship is that it is, essentially, a group mystical experience.

Mystics have always had an equivocal role within the Church. They are not comfortable people. The Roman Church, historically, has often found them tiresome and difficult, and tends to wait until they are safely dead before honouring them. Meanwhile the individual mystic, reared within a certain tradition and valuing it, often struggles with both the church hierarchy and the conventional language and forms of the day. [1]

Contrary to the common view, mystical experience does not lead to a life of pietistic quietude. Indeed, what it seems to bring with it is a sharp, clear perception of things as they actually are. With that comes a powerful urge to either actively

---

[1] Oliver Davies (1988) *God Within: The Mystical Tradition of Northern Europe*

confront and change manifest wrongs, or to stay with what is and strive to create a better mode of functioning. Either path requires courage, and an unsentimental stoicism of purpose.

What of the future for Friends, this unlikely band of non-conformists whose numbers are always threatening to be terminal but in practice are surprisingly constant? More to the point, where will the Spirit lead us?

In the light of recent scandalous events, our sad society could do with Quakers back in their former roles as bankers and enlightened manufacturers. However, that was another age. Our economic recovery, I suspect, will come from the activities of small groups of enthusiastic young people playing around at things that fascinate them — in the way that Microsoft, Apple, and Google came into being. Quakers have their contingent of such lively minded young who will no doubt do their own thing in their own field, come what may.

There is a current social crisis of Care — or more accurately, lack of care.

For many years now Quakers have tended to be drawn from, and involved with the caring and teaching professions. Could we act more collectively in these fields? Thankfully, Quaker schools have managed to keep going against the fashionable trends that have damaged the education system under successive political administrations. Quaker care homes have set an admirable standard of care and kindliness. We could blow our trumpet louder about our achievements in these fields.

I salute the courage of those involved in the field of conflict resolution. Our Peace Witness has provided valuable leadership and impetus in this area. In a world where population pressures are likely to lead to even more open conflict, these skills are going to become ever more needed. Those who have recently been to the Middle East as observers, witnesses, and have come back to tell the tale, have performed a great service. It is no longer possible to ignore the realities behind the political jargon.

Reg Naulty has commented[2] on similarities between Quaker mysticism and the Sufi tradition of Islam. Reading some of the Sufi poets of the 11th -13th centuries — Rumi, Ibn al-Arabi — the voices have a familiar, contemporary ring. Should we be building cultural bridges with the Muslim community based on that shared subjective 'personal experience, ecstasy and a change of character'?

I value my Quaker Meeting as an island of sanity in what all too often feels like a mad and disturbing world. It is such a relief to find myself in a group of ordinary decent folk who have their feet on the ground, yet who can come together to share in that extraordinary experience of the Meeting For Worship. It is a healing encounter.

In just being who we are and doing what we do, we are witnessing to something of great significance. It can look like doing nothing — but it is actually doing something of primary importance — asserting a desperately needed, sane perspective on the world. The code of conduct, any positive action that follows, is secondary to the underlying belief — the way of seeing — based on profound experience. It needs to be treasured and fostered.

---

[2] *The Friend* (February 2nd, 2007)

When the time is right

Perhaps that is all we can do for the time being, all we need to do, until the Spirit moves us collectively in a certain direction. Being, holding, witnessing — these are active behaviours. They are also preparation — for what? We can only wait in readiness.

Hans Kung, the Roman Catholic theologian, has written of the various models of the Christian religion down the ages. He feels that the old forms are now no longer adequate in our current world, and looks forward to yet another formulation, which he calls Paradigm Six. [3]

The Buddhists look forward to the coming of Maitreya — the next incarnation of the Buddha — expected at a time, like now, when religious observance is at a very low ebb.

In our ever more crowded and culturally mixed world, we need a creed which can welcome, embrace and accept those partial but deeply valued religious insights gained over the millennia. Quakerism, because of its absence of dogma and its minimal, flexible ritual is uniquely placed to create a containing spiritual formulation.

Are there any amongst us who can find the words? In a recent article by Hilary Painter,[4] I found the following phrases caught my attention:-

- ' ... healing is integral to Quaker life; . leading a Quaker life is in itself a way of bringing healing to the world ... trying to

---

[3] Kung H. (1994) *Christianity: its essence and history*

[4] *The Friend* (August 9th 2013): 'Healing Ministry'

act from a connection with the Light, the Divine, God, call it what you will, is healing work, whether it be expressed in outward work or more inwardly.'

- ' ...change starts in peoples' hearts; and that change comes by grace.'

- ' ...every Quaker does participate in healing, be it in prayer, a welcoming cup of tea, or many far more concrete works. We all understand the value of doing what Love requires of us.'

It seems to me that all our various Quaker concerns are ultimately attempts to bring healing — to individuals, to groups, into situations of hurt and conflict. All require that *the other* is listened to, is heard; that pain and anger are allowed expression; that the individuals and groups concerned feel understood and confirmed (and not denied) in their experience; and that they are held, contained, and suffered with, until they have had time to assimilate their distress. Only then is it possible to forgive and move on.

The South African experience of Reconciliation has been a remarkable example of what can be done in the most difficult conditions.

Those of us who are less at the sharp end of events, nonetheless, in our daily lives, have the opportunity to behave in ways that can either promote creative living — or block it. We can create a facilitating environment around us — or a depriving one. We are all potential healers. This is a concept — that of the *Ministry of Healing* — around which we, the Religious Society of Friends, could unite, which would give us a sense of our role within the Church, within God's world, whatever the future tribulations and vicissitudes, and whatever the shape of our individual lives.

Postscript

Change is an inexorable given. We live in a world which is endlessly evolving, and we are a part of that evolution. The recurring cycle of birth, life and death goes on at every level, from the stars in the heavens to the smallest living creature, and we cannot escape it.

If it undoubtedly challenges us, it also stimulates us. It is in our response to the challenges that we develop our potential and grow as the unique individuals that we are.

At the same time, as human beings we are all endowed with some basic biological imperatives — the need for appropriate food, for shelter, for safe space in which to rest, sleep, procreate and rear our young. If these needs are not met, we become stressed; and if that stress continues for too long we are damaged, and our lives become distorted.

As individuals we have some freedom of action and initiative in finding these conditions for ourselves. However, as social beings we are all of us caught up in a social network that we cannot always manage or escape. It is the role of our social leaders, our politicians, to monitor the under-pinning of our wider society and ensure that those basic needs are met.

When in 1976 Emmanuel Todd looked at the Russian statistics for infant mortality, he declared that a society that could not keep its children alive was doomed. On the basis of his findings he predicted the downfall of the USSR some years before it actually happened.

In the UK we have a good record vis-a-vis maternal and infant physical health. However, the level of mental ill-health amongst our children and young people is a cause for serious concern. They are said to be the unhappiest young people in Europe. The level of depression, of drug abuse, of self-harm, of anorexia, cannot allow complacency. Something is amiss, and needs to be addressed. Meanwhile the mental health services have been seriously under-funded for a long time. It doesn't help.

Human beings are enormously adaptable, and enormously ingenious in their capacity to live under widely varying conditions. However, viable adaptation takes time, and there are limits to how much individuals, or individual families, can cope with before breaking down.

Our society has organised itself around the nuclear family, while other cultures have extended family systems. This has given us a considerable degree of personal freedom, and allows us to escape from what can be experienced as claustrophobic pressures from our elders and others.

However, it leaves us vulnerable, especially at a time of great social and geographical mobility such as we have experienced in recent decades. We cannot afford the current high rate of family breakdown which impinges most on the vulnerable young, the sick, and the elderly.

There is a crisis of care, a crisis of housing with so many single people looking for their own space. There is an increasing crisis of economic inequality — unacceptable in a wealthy-enough country. There is also a crisis of trust, of hope and of faith, whether this is expressed in religious or secular terms.

We have ahead of us the task of developing a healthier society. The answers are to be found, not in idealistic political fantasies, not in the micro-management beloved of civil servants, nor in the discoveries of brilliant scientific minds — though these have much to offer — but in the hum-drum minutiae of domestic life.

Whether we like it or not, as D. W. Winnicott said, home is where we start from.

#0065 - 210217 - C0 - 210/148/9 - PB - DID1762489